The Little
Red Book
of China
Business

D0064199

To Jindong

The Little Red Book of China Business

8 ESSENTIAL RULES FOR SUCCESS & PROFIT

SHEILA MELVIN

PIATKUS

ஃ *Visit the Piatkus website!*

Piatkus publishes a wide range of best-selling fiction and non-fiction, including books on health, mind, body & spirit, sex, self-help, cookery, biography and the paranormal.

If you want to:

- read descriptions of our popular titles
- buy our books over the Internet
- take advantage of our special offers
- enter our monthly competition
- learn more about your favourite Piatkus authors

VISIT OUR WEBSITE AT: www.piatkus.co.uk

CONTENTS

ACKNOWLEDGMENTS

This book draws broadly upon the wisdom and experience of many people. They include my former colleagues at the U.S.-China Business Council, in particular, Bob Kapp, Rich Brecher, Anne Stevenson-Yang, and Pam Baldinger; the many representatives of Council member companies with whom I was privileged to work; innumerable, and here unnamed but much appreciated, friends and professional acquaintances whom I have been privileged to know over the years in China; my professor at the Johns Hopkins School of Advanced International Studies, Alice Lyman Miller; and my extended family, especially my husband Jindong Cai, my brother-in-law Jinyong Cai, and my sister-in-law Jinqing Cai. Several people were helpful in discussing specific issues that I grappled with as I wrote this, including Kathy Chen, Alex Clegg, Michelle Garnaut, Ed Hotard, Jean-Christophe Iseux, Elizabeth Knup, Corina Larkin, Doug Markel, Charlie Martin, Luke Minford, and Stuart Schonberger. Of course, any errors of fact, omission, or interpretation are mine and mine alone. I would also like to thank my agent, Jill Marsal, and my editor, Peter Lynch, for their work on this project. And, finally, I would like to thank my father, Donald Melvin; my mother, Sarah Campbell; and my sister, Michelle Melvin, for their long support of my love for writing and for

China, and my children, Sebastian and Cecilia, for their burgeoning support of both.

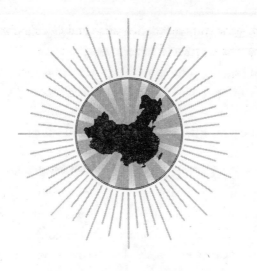

INTRODUCTION:

MAO'S CONTINUING RELEVANCE

We must hold high the great banner of Mao Zedong Thought at all times and under all circumstances...Mao Zedong's emergence in China is the pride of the Communist Party of China, the Chinese people, and the Chinese nation.

—CHINESE PRESIDENT HU JINTAO, IN CELEBRATION OF THE 110TH ANNIVERSARY OF CHAIRMAN MAO ZEDONG'S BIRTH, DECEMBER 26, 2003.

Mao Zedong founded the People's Republic of China and ruled it for twenty-seven years—nearly as long as his successors Deng Xiaoping, Jiang Zemin and Hu Jintao combined. The Mao era may officially be over, but Mao's influence is not. Mao's corpse lies in state in the heart of Beijing because he remains central to the Communist Party's hold on power and to China's vision of itself as a nation. Like it or not, Mao still matters—to China and to you.

Mao matters because the current generation of Chinese leaders was raised under him and governs in a system that he created. Today's leaders have all been affected by his example and his thought and need him to justify the continuation of Communist Party dictatorship—even the much reformed dictatorship that it is today. Keenly aware of this, leaders actively preserve many of Mao's teachings and manipulate his memory in support of their political goals, even as they remain ever vigilant against repeating the catastrophic mistakes of his rule. As the acclaimed China watcher Orville Schell put it, "Just as Mao's portrait has never been taken down from The Gate of Heavenly Peace, so whole elements of his revolution continue to survive in China's institutions, ways of thinking, and modes of interacting with the world. Like recessive genes, they sometimes suddenly re-express themselves." With a working knowledge of Mao's thinking, strategies, and tactics, you will be better able to navigate the Chinese system and you will gain valuable insight into the thinking of the government officials who oversee it.

Mao matters because in ways large and small, positive and negative, everyone in China has been influenced by his person and his thought. Virtually anyone over forty-five can still recite large passages from *The Quotations of Chairman Mao* (better known outside China as "The Little Red Book") in the same rote manner that an American can say the "Pledge of Allegiance." Chinese who were born after Mao's death have not been so directly influenced by his thinking, but they have absorbed it through their parents, their education, and popular culture. They sing songs about Mao in karaoke bars, admire his poetry and calligraphy, and even pay homage to him in an online memorial hall where visitors can post messages and send virtual flowers. A deeper understanding of Mao and his continuing influence will benefit you when it comes to better understanding many of your Chinese colleagues, competitors, customers, and friends.

Mao matters because he was a master of politics, strategy, marketing, organizational management, and many other areas which are essential to your business success in China.

Indeed, Mao is the man who sold the utterly alien philosophy of Communism to the world's most populous nation and then ensured that it took root. Unlike his ancient compatriots, the strategist Sun Tzu and philosopher Lao Tzu—whose works many business people are fond of parsing for advice—Mao both commanded an army and ruled a nation. For better and worse, his ideas were implemented. Mao had experience with startup ventures—the Red Army and the Communist Party—and with bureaucratic monoliths, namely the People's Republic of China. He worked on the line, leading troops in guerrilla warfare, and in the "head shed," crafting policies and strategies. He was an innovator and an iconoclast who ignored conventional wisdom—and headquarters—and stubbornly insisted on implementing the strategies and tactics that he believed would work best.

Although Mao's teachings are no longer a standard part of the school curriculum, they are increasingly used by Chinese corporations and executives who seek to benefit from his experience and insights. Ren Zhengfei, the founder of the global telecommunications company Huawei, calls Mao's "spirit of rebellion" important to developing his company's spirit of innovation and has borrowed Mao's tactic of "using the countryside to encircle the cities" in his successful quest to grab market share. Zong Qinghou, the founder of the soft-drink giant Wahaha, credits Mao with his leadership style. Chen Tianqiao, founder of the online gaming company Shanda—who in 2004 was listed as China's second richest man—cites the "Selected Works of Mao Zedong" as one of his two favorite books. Lenovo founder Liu Chuanzhi credits Mao with his management style and once said, only half in jest, "Legend has its commercial secrets, but not to those who understand Mao's theories." These titans of Chinese industry study Mao because they recognize that there is more to him than the willful dictator whose tragic flaws, unfathomable errors, and outright crimes we Westerners are so familiar with. In Mao's thought and practice, you, too, can find insight and practical advice to help you succeed in what may be the world's most challenging—and important—market.

Finally, Mao matters because he understood China and its people in a way that few others have. His understanding was acquired through years spent studying China's history, working among its people, and actively investigating the "actual situation" in which his fellow countrymen lived and struggled. The uses to which he put his unparalleled understanding of China and his power to influence—or manipulate—its people too often had tragic consequences and will be debated for many years to come. But, his most basic quest was to make China a modern nation and restore it to its former glory while retaining its unique Chinese characteristics. This remains the fundamental goal of his successors and it is widely shared by the Chinese people. Mao was not an aberration of modern Chinese history, but a product of it. If you are going to begin understanding the China

5

of today—and tomorrow—you had best start with Mao Zedong. *The Little Red Book of China Business* will help you on your way.

The Structure of This Book

Each chapter of *The Little Red Book of China Business* begins with a quotation from Chairman Mao. The quotation is followed by an interpretation of how Mao applied—or failed to apply—his own advice. (Disclaimer: The quotations and themes chosen are those that I believe are most useful to understanding China today or to working there; Mao used much the same approach when he studied the Marxist canon and selectively adapted teachings from it. There is much more to Mao than you'll find here, and certainly not all of it is this engaging.)

Mao believed in tempering theory with practice. In this spirit, the lesson from his thought and life is then broadened and applied to contemporary China, and to the situations, problems, and conundrums likely to confront a person doing business there. Each chapter then concludes with "A Crystallization of Collective Wisdom." This is the official phrase currently used to describe Mao's thought, and it aptly describes much of the advice in this book, which is crystallized from the knowledge and experiences that hundreds of business people, diplomats, lawyers, journalists, artists, and ordinary people have shared with me over two decades of working with and writing about China.

Notes

We must hold high the great banner of Mao Zedong Thought—"Hu Jintao Speech at CPC Forum on Mao Zedong's 110th Birth Anniversary," Beijing Xinhua, December 26, 2003 (FBIS translation).

Whole elements of [Mao's] revolution—Orville Schell, "China's Victimization Syndrome," www.Project-Syndicate.org, 2005.

Legend has its commercial secrets—in Tang Yuankai, "Mao Now," *Beijing Review*, December 10, 2006.

CHAPTER 1

VALUE HISTORY

China has grown out of the China of the past; we are Marxist in our historical approach and must not lop off our history. We should sum up our history from Confucius to Sun Yat-sen and take over this valuable legacy.

Mao Zedong was obsessed by the study of history. As a child, he read China's most famous novels again and again until he *"learned many of the stories almost by heart."* At first he read for pure pleasure—he loved to lose himself in romantic adventures like *The Three Kingdoms* and *The Water Margin* and even read them during school, *"covering them up with a Classic when the teacher walked past."* But after devouring these novels for fun, he began to analyze their content and to read them as historic documents.

> *I have read the Dream of the Red Chamber five times. First I read it as a story, and then as history.*

Eventually, he moved on from reading fiction as history to reading history itself. In middle school, he encountered the great Song Dynasty text, *A Comprehensive Mirror for the Aid of Those Who Govern*, which is premised on the idea that understanding the past is the key to managing the present. He would consult this, and other classic histories, throughout his life. He also studied some foreign history especially when, irked by his school's strict regulations and limited curriculum, he dropped out for six months to study on his own in the Hunan Provincial Library.

> *During this period of self-education I read many books, studied world geography and world history.*

There for the first time I saw and studied with great interest a map of the world. I read Adam Smith's The Wealth of Nations, *and Darwin's* Origin of Species, *and a book on ethics by John Stuart Mill. I read the works of Rousseau, Spencer's* Logic, *and a book on law written by Montesquieu. I mixed poetry and romances, and the tales of ancient Greece, with serious study of history and geography of Russia, America, England, France, and other countries.*

In his reading of American history he was impressed by George Washington—long recalling the sentence "After eight years of difficult war, Washington won victory and built up his nation"—and by Benjamin Franklin, who he would remember for rising from poverty to become a writer and "invent electricity." He also learned about Napoleon, who, perhaps unsurprisingly, was his favorite foreign leader.

Naturally, Mao devoted most of his time to the Chinese Classics, studying such works as *The Analects of Confucius*, *The Great Learning*, *The Doctrine of the Mean*, and *The Book of Changes*, that were the basis of traditional education. Mao's father also emphasized the Classics because he considered them practical, having once lost a lawsuit when an adversary used an especially fitting classical quotation against him. Though Mao sometimes chafed against the rigidity of such studies, it did not take him long to realize that his father was right—reading the Classics actually did have practical applications.

> *When I was thirteen I discovered a powerful argument of my own for debating with my father on his ground, by quoting the Classics. My father's favorite accusations against me were of unfilial conduct and laziness. I quoted, in exchange, passages from the Classics saying that the elder must be kind and affectionate. Against his charge that I was lazy I used the rebuttal that older people should do more work than younger, that my father was over three times as old as myself, and therefore should do more work.*

Using the Classics as a weapon against his father apparently worked so well that Mao adopted the practice and used it throughout his life. Indeed, *The Selected Works of Mao Zedong* include five quotations from Confucius for every one quotation from Marx.

Mao continued to study history throughout his life because he loved it and because he knew it was an invaluable tool. As he often told others, *"We have to learn from the past to serve the present."* If this was true for Mao, it is even truer for those of us who are outsiders to Chinese culture, to Communist politics, or to both. The more you understand China's recent past, the better you will comprehend its present; and the better you understand the present, the greater your odds of success in any China-related endeavor.

THE HISTORY OBSESSION

The immense pleasure that Mao took in the study of history is shared by many of his fellow citizens. If you channel surf in China, you will find yourself flipping through countless historic documentaries and docudramas on sometimes narrow topics—like ancient coins or the early years of the Kangxi Emperor—which may run every day for months. Bookstores overflow with history and pop-history books. In 2005, a "de-coding" of "The Dream of the Red Chamber" sold more than half a million copies, and in 2006, it became the topic of a hit reality show in which thousands of people competed to play starring roles in a televised version of the beloved story. In 2006, a university professor's analysis of Confucius' "Analects" had a first print run of 600,000 and sold 10,000 copies in one day—at a single Beijing book signing. "Three Kingdoms"—one of Mao's favorites—was also the subject of a 2003 business book that sold 100,000 copies a month for the better part of a year and of a 2006 essay collection that sold 600,000 copies the first month it was published, As Mao predicted, it is the times of chaos that most people like to read about and watch—including the Mao era itself. To commemorate the thirtieth anniversary of Mao's death in September 2006, bookstores were filled to bursting with new and old Mao-related titles—of which more than 10,000 have reportedly been published in China.

Integration and Humiliation

Your study should at a minimum encompass the past two centuries since this is the era of China's tortuous integration into the international system. A good starting point is 1793 when the British envoy Lord George Macartney sailed to China hoping to establish formal diplomatic relations and sign a treaty of friendship and commerce between Britain and China. Macartney brought lavish gifts for Emperor Qianlong, including a planetarium and a pair of diamond-studded enamel watches, and was accompanied by a ninety-five-man entourage that included a German marching band.

Although the delegation was intended to impress China with Britain's might, Emperor Qianlong prevaricated for weeks before finally receiving Lord Macartney in his imperial audience tent. He treated Macartney politely and hosted him at a banquet so sublime that the awed envoy compared it to the "celebration of a religious mystery." But, when the banquet was over, Emperor Qianlong sent Macartney home with a gift bag of tea and silk, and a letter for King George that is one of the most famous in diplomatic history. It read, in part:

> ...we have never valued ingenious articles, nor do we have slightest need of your country's manufactures. Therefore, O, King, as regards your request to send someone to remain at the capital, while it is not in harmony with the regulations of the Celestial Empire we also feel very much that it is of no advantage to your country. Hence we have issued these detailed instructions and have commanded your tribute envoys to return safely home. You, O King, should simply act in conformity with our wishes by strengthening your loyalty and swearing perpetual obedience so as to ensure that your country may share the blessings of peace.

Emperor Qianlong, in other words, would accept the gifts only as a courtesy and within the rubric of China's traditional tribute system since it was inconceivable for him to deal with King George—or Great Britain—as an equal. But, it was equally inconceivable for the British to "swear perpetual obedience" to the Chinese Empire, or to continue trading within the narrow confines of the tribute system; the British public had become so fond of

Chinese tea that England found itself importing increasingly large amounts while China bought almost nothing from England (a scenario that might sound familiar).

Unable to find any manufactured articles that the Chinese would pay for, British traders hit upon something else: opium. They had easy access to the addictive narcotic in British-controlled India, and traders sold it into China at the southern port of Canton, where they purchased the tea that had become an integral part of British life. This "triangular trade" completely reversed the trade deficit, causing silver to pour out of China and into the coffers of British merchants. It also led to the debilitating addiction of millions of Chinese, from wealthy officials to starving rickshaw pullers. The opium trade helped catapult China into an era of inexorable decline that is nowadays generally summed up in one word: humiliation.

This era of humiliation began in 1838 when the Qing Emperor Daoguang ordered an esteemed official named Lin Zexu to end the devastating opium trade. Commissioner Lin tried to make the British see the evil of their ways, and he even wrote a poignant letter to Queen Victoria that included the fitting question, "Let us ask, where is your conscience?" When persuasion didn't work, he confiscated nearly three million pounds of the traders' opium, dumped it into a trench, mixed it with salt and lime, and flushed it out to sea—having first warned all sea creatures to swim clear of the contamination.

Lin's noble efforts were to no avail, and war broke out in 1839. Although the proud and determined commissioner had failed with diplomacy, he still expected to triumph militarily over the foreign barbarians. So it came as a shock to him—and his boss—when China was resoundingly defeated by the British Navy. An angry Emperor Daoguang blamed Lin for starting the war with his "excessive zeal" and exiled him to the far western region of Xinjiang. "Now, one thousand unending problems are sprouting," the emperor chastised his erstwhile commissioner. "As we think about your grievous failings, we become furious, and then melancholy."

The unending problems which followed the first Opium War were to be more numerous than even Emperor Daoguang could have imagined. They include:

- The 1842 "Treaty of Nanking," which ended the Opium War and forced China to cede Hong Kong to Britain in perpetuity, open five "treaty ports" to foreign trade, and pay a significant indemnity. This was but the first of a series of "unequal treaties" under which the Qing government was forced to relinquish much of its sovereignty to foreign nations, including the United States, France, Russia, and Japan. The Treaty of Nanking and the subsequent "unequal treaties" are considered the start of China's humiliation and decline and subsequently became a key inspiration for the growth of Chinese nationalism.

- The burning of the Yuanmingyuan Summer Palace by French and British troops in 1860 as revenge for the treatment of British prisoners following the Second Opium War (1856–1860). Yuanmingyuan was once one of the most magnificent palace-garden complexes in the world, the Chinese equivalent of Versailles. Its vast gardens contained fountains, temples, palaces—including several designed in European style by Jesuit missionaries—priceless art collections, a botanical garden, the imperial zoo, and the nation's most important library. "You can scarcely imagine the beauty and magnificence of the palaces we burnt," wrote a British participant. "It made one's heart sore...it was wretchedly demoralizing work for an army." The ruins of Yuanmingyuan are today both a park and a potent reminder of China's past humiliation. The sign at the entrance reads: 'Do not forget the national shame, rebuild the Chinese nation."

- The Boxer Rebellion and the Eight Powers attack on Beijing in 1900. The Boxers were an anti-Christian, anti-foreign movement whose mainly rural members practiced qigong and believed themselves invulnerable to bullets and swords. They gained widespread popularity beginning in 1899 and even won the support of the Empress Dowager who hoped to use them to rid China of foreign imperialists. But in 1900 the Boxers occupied Beijing, killing several hundred foreigners and tens of thousands of Chinese Christians. This led the eight foreign powers with major interests in China, among them the United States and Britain, to muster an army and defeat the Boxers. The Chinese government was forced to pay the eight powers an enormous indemnity equivalent to $333 million in U.S. dollars. (The U.S. used part of its indemnity to establish what is now the renowned Tsinghua University, which began as a preparatory school for Chinese students who wished to study in the U.S.)

- The end of the Qing Dynasty, the establishment of the Republic of China in 1911, and years of civil war. The humiliating defeat by the eight powers spurred the imperial government to undertake many reforms—including the 1905 abolishment of the imperial exam system by which officials had been chosen for 1300 years—but these ultimately proved to be too little, too late. The Qing Dynasty—and the entire dynastic system—collapsed in 1911 and was replaced by the Republic of China, with Dr. Sun

Yat-sen as its first president. Dr. Sun's party, the Nationalists, struggled to consolidate their power and rule for many years even as warlords controlled great sections of the country. After Dr. Sun's death, General Chiang Kai-shek became the Nationalist Party leader, intermittently battling the Communist Party for control of China until the Communist victory in 1949, when he led 2 million of his soldiers and fellow Nationalists in retreat to Taiwan.

• The devastating Japanese invasion and occupation. Japan occupied the northeast section of China known as Manchuria in the early 1930s because it desired its abundant raw materials and wanted a buffer to the Soviet Union. War officially broke out in July of 1937 when Japanese and Chinese soldiers battled at Marco Polo Bridge on the outskirts of Beijing, which was soon occupied. Shanghai fell by autumn, and in December, Japanese troops occupied the Nationalist capital of Nanjing, where by some estimates they raped and murdered 300,000 civilians and committed such unspeakable atrocities as tossing infants into the air and catching them on the tips of bayonets. The Nationalist and Communist armies joined together to battle the Japanese, who finally surrendered in September of 1945 after the U.S. dropped atomic bombs on Hiroshima and Nagasaki. The number of military and non-military Chinese deaths during the "War of Resistance Against Japan" is estimated between 20 and 35 million. The cruelty of some Japanese soldiers and the ongoing refusal of some right-wing Japanese nationalists to acknowledge their nation's war crimes continues to negatively affect the China-Japan relationship.

Over the course of just one century, China went from perceiving itself as the "celestial nation" to being seen by others as the "sick man of Asia." The "grievous failings" that reduced it to this state—certainly not Lin Zexu's alone—were resoundingly redressed in 1949 when Mao Zedong declared, *"The Chinese people have stood up!"* and founded the People's Republic of China, putting an end to years of foreign imperialism and civil war. But, like Emperor Daoguang, China still feels both furious and melancholy whenever it revisits this era in its history.

One might reasonably imagine that it would have increasingly few occasions to do so. It is, after all, the world's fastest growing economy and a respected, even envied, member of the international community. But, in fact, this *"semi-colonial, semi-feudal"* history of humiliation is drilled into children starting in middle school and is regularly reinforced through the government propaganda machine. Any commemoration of a major political holiday—or even of some barely-remembered "humiliating" incident—is certain to be accompanied by a spate of related television documentaries and newspaper editorials. A piece that ran in the Communist Party newspaper *People's Daily* on the eve of National Day 2005, for instance, noted that although China had five thousand years of history, its "real" development only began on October 1, 1949 because that day marked the start of the Chinese people's "freedom, once and for all, from humiliation and starvation."

> For a whole century before the late Chairman Mao Zedong pronounced the birth of New China, the Chinese nation was tormented by foreign invasions and wars fought among warlords for supremacy over the country. The humiliation the nation suffered was so bitter that Deji Cholga, a seventh grader...says she hates to study that part of Chinese history.

> The part of the nation's history the teenage girl feels unpleasant to learn covered the Opium War (1840), in which the United Kingdom, with just 20,000 troops and fifty gunboats, defeated the antiquated armies of the Qing (1644–1911), China's last feudal dynasty, which boasted 900,000 men...Even more bitter were memories of Japanese aggression against China...

"In the 200 years from 1750 to 1950," says Prof. Hu Angang of the prestigious Tsinghua University in Beijing, "much of the world was striving for industrialization, but the Chinese economy stood stagnant, and the country was rated as one of the weakest in the world."

China has many good reasons for being angry about its treatment at the hands of the Western nations who carved its coastal cities into semi-colonies and the Japanese who tried to conquer it, slaughtering untold millions of innocent civilians in the process. One of Mao Zedong's greatest achievements was to make people feel, on a visceral level, the unfairness of their victimization at the hands of "*imperialists, warlords, corrupt officials, local tyrants and evil gentry*" and then direct their rightful anger into political and military channels that enabled China to defeat Japan and the Communists to triumph over the Nationalists.

"We can rally the overwhelming majority of the people to fight with one heart and one mind because we are the oppressed and the victims of aggression," he explained.

Unfortunately, the tactic proved so effective for motivating, unifying and channeling discontent that Mao continued to use it. On the eve of victory in 1949, he codified the official view of China's modern history as one of victimization at the hands of outsiders when he explained in a now-famous speech, *"The Chinese have always been a great, courageous, and industrious people. It was only in modern times that they have fallen behind, and this was due solely to the oppression and exploitation of foreign imperialism and the domestic reactionary government."*

Once the imperialists, warlords, corrupt officials, local tyrants and evil gentry had all been expelled, executed, or reformed, Mao created outsiders within China on whom problems could be blamed. These "enemies of the people" were isolated from society at large with labels such as *rightists, capitalist-roaders, stinking intellectuals, ghosts, monsters,* and *snake spirits* that served as verbal prisons. The majority of *"good people"* were then permitted to blame, abuse, and attack the despised minority. The *"good people"* needed little encouragement to attack the *"enemies,"* since Chinese society was rife with festering resentments, and Mao's word was taken as dogma.

After Mao's death, the Communist Party largely rejected the strategy of creating enemies within, but has continued to keep alive the strong sense of victimization that brought it to power. The contrast between the humiliations of the past and the achievements of the present presumably offers a compelling justification for its continued monopoly on power. It is also convenient to blame outsiders—British colonists, American hegemonists, Japanese rightists, hostile Western forces attempting to 'Westernize' and 'disintegrate' China, Taiwan splittists—for diplomatic disturbances, social ills, sexually transmitted diseases, or just plain old tough times. Although this sense of victimization is deliberately cultivated, it has strong historic roots and is very real. It will continue to affect China's interaction with the outside world—especially with the West and Japan—in diplomacy, commerce, and even personal relationships for the foreseeable future.

Standing Up—and Struggling— Under Chairman Mao

When it comes to the post-1949 era, the best prism through which to view Chinese history is: Mao Zedong. As Mao wrote in his youth, *"In order to grasp the outline and ascertain the details pertaining to the entire duration of a dynasty, there is no better way than to seek out its greatest and most powerful men. Great and powerful men are representatives of an era, and by assembling one by one every single piece of evidence relating to their lives, one will see that the whole era is but an accessory to these representative people."*

For as long as the People's Republic of China lasts, Mao Zedong will always be its most representative figure. It is too soon to know if all PRC history will one day be judged as accessory to Mao, but it is safe to say that much of its first five decades can be viewed this way. Using Mao as an historic prism, there are many refracted themes one could follow, but perhaps the most interesting is that of faith—Mao's faith in the masses and the masses' faith in Mao.

Mao believed firmly in the *"boundless"* power and *"potentially inexhaustible enthusiasm"* of the masses to build socialism and transform China. His belief was strengthened by China's military victory over Japan in 1945 and by the Red Army's triumph over the Nationalist Army in 1949, since both were examples of a militarily inferior army triumphing over a vastly superior force with the support of the masses. The involvement of the masses of Chinese people was thus crucial to his ideology. As he put it:

> ...*all correct leadership is necessarily "from the masses, to the masses." This means: "take the ideas of the masses (scattered and unsystematic ideas) and concentrate them (through study turn them into concentrated and systematic ideas), then go to the masses and propagate and explain these ideas until the masses embrace them as their own, hold fast to them and translate them into action, and test the correctness of these ideas in such action."*

This process was to go on "over and over again in an endless spiral, with the ideas becoming more correct, more vital and richer each time.

Mao's faith in the masses was certainly instrumental in China's transformation from a weak, divided, and war-torn nation into a global power with nuclear weapons and, by the end of Mao's life, a permanent seat on the UN Security Council. But it also meant that his tenure at the helm of the PRC was an endless spiral of mass movements and political campaigns in which the vast majority of Chinese were obliged to participate whether they liked it or not.

This campaign style of government happened to play to Mao's strengths—his great skills were as a peasant organizer and a revolutionary leader, and he detested bureaucracy. He believed that it was necessary to light political fires every few years so that human beings could be "*tempered*," just like steel, and even in peacetime he stressed such concepts as "*continuing revolution*" and "*class struggle*." As he put it in a youthful poem, "*One draws endless pleasures from struggling against the soil, and against other people.*"

The problem, of course, is that most people do not draw endless pleasure from struggling against each other; where Mao thrived in chaos, his fellow Chinese dreaded it.

IN PRAISE OF CHAOS

As a young man in 1917–1918, Mao Zedong read *A System of Ethics* by the German philosopher Friedrich Paulsen. In his margin notes, next to a discussion of "good and evil," he penned this intriguing comment:

> *Since the earliest of times, when a period of order is followed by a period of chaos, human beings always hate the chaos and hope for order, not realizing that chaos too is part of the process of historical life, that it too has value in real life. When we read history, we always praise the era of the Warring States...the era of the struggles among the Three Kingdoms. It is the times when things are constantly changing, and numerous men of talent are emerging, that people like to read about. When they come to periods of peace, they are bored and put the book aside. It is not that we like chaos, but simply that the reign of peace cannot last long, is unendurable to human beings, and that human nature is delighted by sudden change.*

Early mass movements associated with land reform, marriage reform, agricultural collectivization, and nationalization of industry had seemingly widespread support. People could see that after years of war, occupation, inflation, and starvation, life was finally getting better. Indeed, the early 1950s are often cited as a kind of golden age of unity, honesty, and purpose even by people who later suffered immensely.

But, by 1957, when Mao launched the Hundred Flowers Campaign, some were already weary of political movements. The Hundred Flowers was intended to encourage intellectuals to freely critique the Communist Party's work, and among the many complaints ultimately voiced was the excessive number of political movements. This sort of criticism was not what Mao had expected to hear, and the Hundred Flowers was brought to a hasty end with the full support of his fellow leaders, who had never approved of it in the first place. It was followed by the Anti-Rightist Movement in which those who had spoken out at Mao's bidding were persecuted as "rightists" with half a million intellectuals condemned, exiled, or sent to labor camps. Deng Xiaoping was in charge of running the campaign, which included a quota system that required most work units to deem five percent of their employees "rightist." (Deng's close involvement no doubt partly explains why, half a century later, the Communist Party still refuses to officially repudiate the movement or make compensation to its victims.)

If Mao had been upset by the blunt criticisms of the Party voiced in the Hundred Flowers, he himself was also growing increasingly critical of his fellow leaders' apparent zest for bureaucratization and insistence on copying from the Soviet Union. Mao was also disappointed by low agricultural production figures and the peasants' increasing *"individualism,"* or desire for higher living standards. Loath to see his revolution bogged down by bureaucracy and self-interest, he decided to jump start it with a Great Leap Forward in 1958. Through sheer will power and collective effort, China would radically increase the productivity of both agriculture and industry, surpassing Britain's level of steel production in three years.

To achieve this grandiose goal, peasant households were organized into huge "people's communes" in which everything was shared. A hundred million peasants worked together on public irrigation projects while around the country steel was smelted in "backyard furnaces." Great Leap euphoria—or lunacy—soon extended to every area of life, with even symphony orchestras pledging to perform thousands of concerts per year, all in the service of Mao's utopian vision. While agricultural production did increase, able-bodied men were so busy smelting home-made steel (much of which proved unusable) that they could not bring in all of the bumper harvest. This, and the fact that local officials lied to meet inflated production quotas, meant that the nation was utterly unable to cope when bad weather struck large parts of the country in 1959 and 1960. A famine of incomprehensible magnitude resulted, with between 16 and 40 million people starving to death, most of them peasants, even as China continued to export grain.

This was certainly not the intended outcome of

Mao's vision for the Great Leap, and he went into political and personal retreat for a time, and even gave up eating meat during the famine. But he did not alter his faith in the power of the masses to transform China according to his vision—or his belief that it still needed to be transformed. The masses, most of whom were (and are still) unaware of the scale of famine, also remained faithful to Mao. In 1963, the sycophantic Defense Minister Lin Biao (who would turn traitor in 1971) compiled a little red book of Mao's aphorisms called *Quotations from Chairman Mao* and required soldiers to study it, thereby deepening the already great sense of Mao as a mythic figure.

But within the leadership, Mao's position had been weakened enough that when he proposed launching another mass movement, he faced opposition from colleagues who did not want to disrupt the nation's recovery. Mao responded by charging that his opponents lacked faith in the masses and, in 1966, Mao unleashed the Cultural Revolution, the biggest mass movement of them all. The goals of the Cultural Revolution were never clearly spelled out, but included combating bureaucracy, capitalism, old customs, old culture, old habits and old thinking. It was also a factional struggle that enabled Mao's wife, Jiang Qing, and three other leftists to assume great power.

The result was a state of turmoil which lasted several

years and in which hundreds of thousands of innocent people—intellectuals, teachers, musicians, former Nationalists, former capitalists—were humiliated, tortured, and sometimes killed by mobs of "revolutionary" Red Guards. Some argue that Mao did not directly order the murder and destruction in the early years of the Cultural Revolution, but nor did he intervene to stop it until the nation was on the brink of anarchy. Though old and sick in his final years, Mao knew that his final revolution had not succeeded. *"What will happen to the next generation if it all fails?"* he asked. *"There may be a foul wind and a rain of blood. How will you cope? Heaven only knows!"*

As we all know, his successors have coped remarkably well. Led by Deng Xiaoping, they began by abandoning Mao's pet themes of class struggle, continuing revolution, and mass movements. Deng de-emphasized ideology, arguing that "it doesn't matter if the cat is black or white as long as it catches the mouse." He freed farmers to grow their own grain and opened up the private economy, describing the resulting mixture of public and private ownership as "socialism with Chinese characteristics." But, while Deng and his fellow leaders discarded many of Mao's policies, they did not abandon the man himself.

On the contrary, the official 35,000 word verdict on Party history issued under Deng's guidance declares

Comrade Mao Zedong was a great Marxist and

a great proletarian revolutionary, strategist and theorist. It is true that he made gross mistakes during the "cultural revolution," but, if we judge his activities as a whole, his contributions to the Chinese revolution far outweigh his mistakes. His merits are primary and his errors secondary.

In reaching this assessment, Deng neatly followed Mao's guidance as illustrated in the quote that appears at the beginning of this chapter—he summed up the Party's history and preserved Mao's "valuable legacy" for the Party's continued use. As he put it,

The banner of Mao Zedong Thought can never be discarded. To throw it away would be nothing less than to negate the glorious history of our Party...It would be ill-advised to say too much about Comrade Mao Zedong's errors. To say too much would be to blacken Comrade Mao, and that would blacken the country itself. That would go against history.

And so it is that to understand China's present, we must still come to terms with Mao Zedong.

WOLF'S MILK?

The "humiliation" and "victimization" version of

33

modern Chinese history is likely to remain standard for some time, but a growing number of bold critics have begun to question its validity—and its usefulness.

One of these is historian Yuan Weishi, who in a 2006 essay called, "Modernization and History Textbooks," charged that modern history as presented in Chinese textbooks is "wolf's milk" that is full of inaccuracies and misrepresentations intended to blame foreigners and exculpate China. He decried the need to demonstrate patriotism by always assuming that China is right in any conflict and cherry-picking from historical materials, using only those "that favor China whether they are true or false." Instead, he argued, all historical materials should be analyzed rationally and selected for their veracity, concluding:

> ...In an era of rapid globalization, conflicts of interest among corporations and nations are unavoidable. Rational understanding and resolving conflicts is the best choice for any nation or corporation. If anything related to the outside is always about "anti-imperialism" and "anti-hegemony," then the matter is bound to be bungled.

The appearance of Professor Yuan's seven-thousand-plus-word article in the magazine "Freezing Point" caused such a stir that the publication was shut down for rectification and then forced to run what was essentially a retraction. But the door to further debate remains open.

Li Datong, the Communist Party member who edited *Freezing Point* for eleven years until he was relieved of his duty, argued that the article caused so much consternation because "the Party's legitimacy must now be followed all the way to the writing of official history." He noted that this official history therefore largely eliminates such tragedies as the Great Leap Forward famine because this could cause people to ask too many questions.

> ...the moment other versions of history are allowed, the legitimacy of the party will be questioned. The first question will be: What government could allow 40 million people to starve and die, never tell about it, but still survive? The main issue is—who holds the...authority to say what history really means.

A CRYSTALLIZATION OF COLLECTIVE WISDOM

We'll now explore some of the ways in which under-standing China's history—and Mao's approach to it—can directly benefit your work in China.

- **USE THE PAST TO ANALYZE THE PRESENT.**

  Knowledge of Chinese history—and the official interpretation of this history—is the best way to understand China. It will help you to recognize the sensitivities of its government and people, predict the response to certain situations, and react. Close students of Chinese history, for example, were not sur-prised when NATO's accidental 1999 bombing of the Chinese embassy in Belgrade enraged the Chinese government and led to massive anti-U.S. demonstra-tions and the torching of a U.S. consular residence, because they understood that it would be interpreted not as a tragic mistake, but as yet another humiliation at the hands of a Western power.

- **BE READY FOR EMOTIONAL OUTPOURINGS.**

  Deliberate emotionalism was an important part of Mao's political rule, and its influence still lingers in PRC diplomacy and politics. "You have hurt the feel-ings of the Chinese people" is a common official response to an untoward diplomatic event, and vitriolic tongue-lashings often follow. Former Hong Kong governor Chris Patten was called a "sinner of a thousand years," a "prostitute," and a "tango-dancer" during the run-up to the 1997 Hong Kong handover. Former Taiwan president Li Teng-hui fared even worse, variously labeled "a rat running across the street," "the number one scum in the nation," and "a deformed test-tube baby." You are unlikely to hear such spectacularly colorful language, but you may well have more run-of-the-mill vitriol directed at your nation in a time of great tension.

- **BE READY FOR PERSONALIZED BLAME.**

Historic events—both past and current—are often personalized, and it is common for foreigners in China to be challenged with historic "you" statements. I have been told, by people as different as a Beijing cab driver and a powerful mayor: "You burned Yuanmingyuan," "You bombed our embassy," and "You sent missionaries to China to destroy our traditional culture." In times of diplomatic crisis, individual foreigners may be lectured for hours by Chinese customers or government counterparts, denied official meetings, singled out for blame by Chinese students, refused rides by cab drivers, or—in rare cases—physically threatened.

37

- **BE PREPARED FOR COLLATERAL DAMAGE WHEN DIPLOMACY GOES AWRY.**

This emotional personalization of historic events, past and present, means you must prepare to protect your organization and your employees—both foreign and Chinese—in the event of a diplomatic crisis. Some American businesses and individuals were targets in the aftermath of the Belgrade bombing in 1999, as were Japanese in the 2005 anti-Japan protests. To defuse the negative impact of the bombing, American companies held meetings at which Chinese and American employees could vent; provided statements of sympathy for Chinese employees to read when they were criticized for working for an "American hegemonist" company; and wrote letters expressing regret over the loss of innocent life. Your China crisis management team must be prepared to anticipate and mitigate crises that are provoked as much by historic sensibilities as present realities—and to do this, its members must know their history.

- **RESPECT PRC SOVEREIGNTY—OR ELSE.**

The passage of time and the establishment of an indisputably strong and sovereign China have only recently begun to alter China's sense of itself as weak and vulnerable. Safeguarding sovereignty at all costs still remains one of its chief diplomatic goals and explains its continued opposition to "interference in the internal affairs" of other nations, even in dire situations. Any action that can be interpreted as impinging upon or questioning China's sovereignty will elicit a strong negative reaction. This could include leaving Taiwan off a map of China on product packaging; dropping the "People" from People's Republic when greeting the PRC president on the White House lawn; or even just assuming that you have a right to be in China (when all you really have are privileges granted you by the sovereign Chinese state). Extra caution and sensitivity must be used when dealing with any subject that could conceivably relate to China's sense of sovereignty. This is especially true of highly public endeavors—like advertising or PR work—but it also applies to internal company communications and conversations. If you have a strong sense of history you will be able to anticipate sensitive areas—and it is always wise to confirm your judgment with others, especially trusted, history-wise locals.

- **USE HISTORY TO YOUR ADVANTAGE.**
Some organizations are fortunate in that they have a long and positive history in China—and smart in that they have used their history and experience wisely. The American insurance company AIG was founded

in Shanghai in 1919—and in 1992, it became the first foreign insurance company granted a license to do business in China. General Motors sold China's last emperor his first cars (a Buick sedan and limousine) in 1924—and in 1997 beat out Ford in a heated competition to form a joint venture with Shanghai Automotive, which became China's top auto seller in 2005. In 1854, Yale University granted the first American university degree earned by a Chinese student; in 2006, Yale was honored with a visit from President Hu Jintao and also became the only foreign university allowed to trade domestic stocks and bonds in China. If you have a positive history in China, use it; if you don't, build one for the future.

- **BEWARE UNINTENDED HISTORIC ALLUSIONS.**
Historic sensitivity is so strong that it may be directed at seemingly unconnected statements or policies. Microsoft Chairman Bill Gates was quoted in 1998 saying that he was not bothered by China's use of pirated Microsoft software because users would become "addicted" and one day buy it. The comment was immediately associated with the opium addiction of centuries past and caused considerable anger. An American technology company in China was equally oblivious when it implemented a global evaluation policy requiring that five percent of all

employees be put on an improvement-needed watch list. The policy invoked deep resentment among employees because the five percent quota and the assumption of wrongdoing evoked memories of the Anti-Rightist Movement, which is what the policy was dubbed by local staff and management. An American bank was fortunate to avoid a similar mistake when a history-wise American executive looked closely at an old photo of its Shanghai headquarters included in promotional materials for an upcoming anniversary—and realized it showed People's Liberation Army soldiers nationalizing the bank in 1949. Since the bank intended to commemorate its long and illustrious history in China—not the rather less glorious chapter of its forced take-over and decades-long expulsion from the China market—the executive quickly pulled the materials. So first learn your history, and then use your knowledge to prevent your company from unintentionally alienating its Chinese customers, employees, and official contacts—or just plain embarrassing itself.

• **BE ON GUARD FOR HISTORIC REFERENCES.**
It has long been politically and culturally impolitic to make direct criticisms in China—particularly if your target is the government. Instead people "use the past to criticize the present." Mao Zedong was convinced

that an opera about an honest Ming Dynasty official who upbraided the emperor was really aimed at him; Deng Xiaoping was likewise said to have believed that a movie about China's first emperor, who is infamous for killing scholars, was intended as a rebuke to him in the wake of the June 4, 1989 killings of student demonstrators and other unarmed civilians. You too should tune your ear to historic references. If, for example, you find a government official lecturing you about the Opium War or the burning of Yuanmingyuan, you had better assume it to be a veiled criticism and dig to find out what current policy of your company or nation is being referenced. And if your partner suddenly starts referring to your contract as an "unequal treaty," watch out.

- **HISTORIC AND CULTURAL SENSITIVITY WINS POINTS.**
Respect for Chinese history and culture will serve you and your corporation well. AIG demonstrated this when it used its philanthropic wing, the Starr Foundation, to purchase carved doors that had been looted from the Summer Palace during the Boxer Rebellion. It returned the looted doors to China as a gift in 1993 and received considerable acclaim and publicity. China's own Poly Group spent nearly 4 million in U.S. dollars to purchase three bronze animal heads that had once adorned a fountain in Yuanmingyuan.

The heads were being sold at auction in Hong Kong in 2000—over loud objections from Beijing. (The auctioneers, Christie's and Sotheby's, displayed a stunning lack of historical sensitivity.) Poly's savvy move brought it reams of free publicity—*People's Daily* called it "a knight in bronze armor"—and major political kudos. The French regularly get extra credit for historic and cultural appreciation. A 2004 *People's Daily* article admiringly described the "China Complexes" of each French president from De Gaulle to Chirac. Jacques Chirac got the most points for examining a photo of a Chinese bronze and asking, "Is this from the third period of the Erlitou Culture?" According to *People's Daily*, Chirac's insightful question "struck dumb" a Chinese bronze expert and remains "a widespread story in the field of diplomacy." To stand out from the crowds, develop a strong appreciation of China's rich history and culture and share it with others both informally and through corporate support of (non-controversial) cultural and historic endeavors.

• **APPROPRIATE CHINESE HISTORY AND CULTURE WITH CAUTION.**

Admiring Chinese culture is good; using it for your own purposes is risky. Toyota and Nippon Paint both ran into trouble in 2004 when they ran commercials using Chinese symbols. The Toyota commercial showed two stone lions bowing to a Toyota SUV while the Nippon ad depicted a dragon slipping down a newly painted pole—both were intended to be humorous, but instead were deemed insulting by a number of vocal Chinese viewers. In 2006, Nike and KFC ran into similar problems. Nike's ad showed an NBA star running circles around a cartoon kung fu master, and KFC's a legendary Daoist figure praising a chicken burger. The State Administration of Radio, Film and Television charged that Nike had offended China's "national dignity" while KFC was criticized for not honoring China's history and culture.

- **NEGATIVE HISTORY CAN BE OVERCOME.**
When Hu Jintao visited the U.S. in 2006, he stopped in Seattle to dine at the home of Bill Gates. Former Hong Kong Governor Chris Patten has been forgiven his sins of a thousand years and is regularly quoted in the Chinese press; he spent part of 2006 in China plugging his latest book. Even the British corporation Jardine Matheson—which was founded in Canton and made its fortune selling opium—has built a strong and diversified China business. The Chinese have a strong sense of history—and an equally strong sense of pragmatism.

NOTES:

China has grown out of—in "The Role of the Chinese Communist Party in the National War," October 1938.

learned many of the stories almost by heart—in Edgar Snow, "Red Star Over China," p. 133.

covering them up with a Classic—in Snow, p. 133.

I have read the Dream of the Red Chamber—in Stuart Schram, *Chairman Mao Talks to the People*, p. 223.

During this period of self-education—in Snow, p. 144.

After eight years of difficult war—in Snow, p. 138.

When I was thirteen I discovered—in Snow, p. 132.

The Selected Works of Mao Zedong include five quotations from Confucius—see Lucian Pye, p. 240.

We have to learn from the past to serve—in Li Zhisui, *The Private Life of Chairman Mao*, p. 122.

celebration of a religious mystery—in Lord George Macartney, *An Embassy to China*, p. 123.

we have never valued ingenious articles— in Macartney, *An Embassy to China*, p. 340.

Now, one thousand unending problems are sprouting—in Paul Chrastina, "Emperor of China Declares War on Drugs," opioids.com

For a whole century before—in *People's Daily*, September 30, 2005 (English edition, online).

imperialists, warlords, corrupt officials—in "Report on an Investigation of the the Peasant Movement in Hunan," March 1927.

We can rally the overwhelming majority—in "Problems of Strategy in China's Revolutionary War," December 1936.

The Chinese have always been a great—in "The Chinese People Have Stood Up," September, 1949.

In order to grasp the outline—in "Letter to Xiao Zisheng," September 6, 1915, in *Road to Power*, Volume I, p. 77.

all correct leadership is necessarily—in "Some Questions Concerning Methods of Leadership," June 1, 1943.

over and over again in an endless spiral—in "Some Questions Concerning Methods of Leadership," June 1, 1943.

One draws endless pleasures—in Lucien W. Pye, *Mao Tse-tung: The Man in the Leader*, p. 274.

What will happen to the next generation—in Jonathan Spence, *Mao Zedong*, p. 178.

The banner of Mao Zedong Thought can—in Geremie R. Barmé, "History for the Masses" (from Jonathan Unger, ed., *Using the Past to Serve the Present*, M.E. Sharpe, Inc., Armonk, NY, 1993).

...In an era of rapid globalization—in "Bingdian Article Criticizes PRC Textbooks Views on Boxer Uprising; Japan Cited" "Bingdian" special article by Zhongshan University Professor Yuan Weishi: "Modernization and History Textbooks," *Zhongguo Qingnian Bao, Saturday, January 28, 2006.*

The moment other versions of history are allowed—in Robert Marquand, "China's Media Censorship Rattling World," *Christian Science Monitor*, February 24, 2006.

Since the earliest of times—in Stuart R. Schram, Editor. Mao's *Road to Power, Revolutionary Writings 1912–1949*. Volume I, The Pre-Marxist Period, 1912–1920. Armonk: M.E. Sharpe, 1992, p. 238.

47

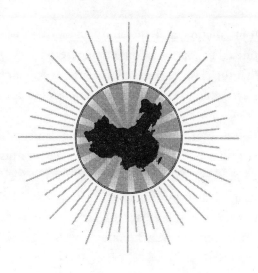

CHAPTER TWO

THE UNITY OF OPPOSITES

The law of the unity of opposites is the fundamental law of the universe. This law operates universally, whether in the natural world, in human society, or in man's thinking. Between the opposites in a contradiction there is at once unity and struggle, and it is this that impels things to move and change.

Contradiction and the unity of opposites—or the idea that contradictions are inherent in everything, and that the clash of these contradictions will ultimately cause everything to change into its opposite—are essential tenets of Mao Zedong Thought.

The unity of opposites is also a fundamental law of Marxist dialectics, together with such confusingly-named principles as the "negation of the negation," and "the transformation of quantity into quality." But Mao emphasized the supremacy of contradictions and the unity of opposites over the other laws from early on in his communist career.

Some scholars speculate that his emphasis on the unity of opposites is due to the many contradictions he saw in Chinese society and the strong influence of Daoist thought. The most recognizable symbol of Daoism, of course, is the yin-yang symbol which represents opposing forces—light and dark, good and evil, male and female—that cannot exist without each other. Under Daoism, there is unity in diversity and harmony is achieved through the reconciliation of opposites.

That this would have influenced Mao's thinking certainly makes sense. But I also suspect that he found the concept of the unity of opposites appealing in part because of his own contradictory nature. Mao was a peasant and an intellectual, a philosopher and soldier, an idealist and a realist, a poet and a pedant, a liberator and an oppressor, a feminist and a womanizer—and the list goes on. He didn't just preach the paramount significance of contradiction and the unity of opposites, he lived it.

Some of the contradictions that Mao embodied in his life and his leadership are small. As a teenager, he loved to read so much that he quit school to go to the library. As a young revolutionary, he had his jackets specially tailored with extra large pockets so he could carry a book with him wherever he went. At the end of his life he lived in a study in which "Manuscripts lined bookshelves along every wall; books covered the table and the floor; it looked more the retreat of a scholar than the audience room of the all-powerful leader of the world's most populous nation." Yet this same Mao regularly advised against the harmful effect of reading too many books.

The more books one reads the more stupid one gets.

Other of Mao's contradictory stances are less innocent. For instance, in 1957 he said,

I think our attitude should be one of unity towards every comrade, no matter who, provided he is not a hostile element or a saboteur...Lenin once said that there is not a single person in the world who does not make mistakes. Everyone needs support.

But while Mao was making this speech in Moscow, the Anti-Rightist campaign back home was destroying the lives of countless intellectuals whose "mistakes" were nothing more than speaking out as he had asked. During the Cultural Revolution, the entire country was thrown into chaos and millions more suffered because Mao—the man who lived in the imperial palace surrounded by ancient books and insisted that China not forget its legacy—decided it was time to destroy much of that very legacy. He prepared to launch the Cultural Revolution by studying an ancient Han Dynasty history—just the sort of book that was thrown into bonfires once the turmoil was underway.

If Mao was contradictory, so is the People's Republic of China—and many of its paramount contradictions were either created or exacerbated by Mao himself. Learning to reconcile (or at least to accept) China's many opposites is an essential part of learning to work with it; the sooner you can do this, the better off you'll be.

This is not an easy task. When Mao looked at China as a young man who had not yet discovered Marxism, even he saw opposites without unity. *"With twenty-two existing provinces, three special areas, and two frontier regions, making twenty-seven regions in all, it would be better to divide China into twenty-seven countries,"* he wrote in 1920.

China indeed is a nation of fifty-six distinct ethnic groups most of whom have absolutely nothing other than geography in common. Even members of the Han majority speak different languages, eat different foods, observe different customs, profess somewhat different values, and generally claim to not like each other very much. Mao came from Hunan—a province known for its spicy food and stubborn people—and was so convinced that he and his fellow Hunanese got *"more harm than good"* from being part of China that he urged them to *"stand up for independence."*

> *"I oppose the 'Great Republic of China,' and advocate a 'Republic of Hunan,'"* he stated boldly.

It was while working for Hunan independence that he first discovered Lenin's writings. Soon thereafter, Mao became a Marxist, accepted the validity of dialectics, and stopped arguing that China should be broken up. Instead, he adopted an opposite tactic, working to unify China under the Communist Party through years of warfare and then, after the 1949 victory, developing a highly centralized state modeled after the Soviet Union. Under Mao's rule, the government behemoth grew until it exercised authority over most of the nation's political, economic, social, and even private life.

But, Mao was never fully comfortable with the bureaucracy his Party established and did not forget his earlier views on the importance of regional autonomy.

"The localities have the right to resist all impracticable, unrealistic, and subjectivist orders, directives, instructions, and forms which the various ministries of the Central Government may send down to them," he declared in 1956. He also encouraged the provinces to be economically independent, even autarkic, so that Chinese industry would not be wiped out if the nation were attacked.

A Difficult Balancing Act

The appropriate balance between unity and disunity in governance was a contradiction that Mao never resolved. His successors have done better, but China is still centralized and decentralized, autocratic and anarchic, governed by alternating—and frequently inconsistent—methods of tension and laxity.

To accommodate the diversity of its immense population, for example, China has five autonomous regions, thirty autonomous prefectures, 117 autonomous counties and even three autonomous "banners" for Mongolians. But in reality, these supposedly autonomous areas have almost no authority to create laws or policies that suit their unique circumstances. Instead, like all provinces, they must depend on the central government for permission to develop and innovate. The classic example of this is the requirement that all China—which spans 5200 kilometers from east to west—keep time by Beijing's clock. In the far west Xinjiang Autonomous

Region, ethnic minorities generally obey the sun and change the clock two hours, while Han Chinese obey the government and do not. This means that any single event—say, the departure of a bus—occurs at two different times depending on the ethnic background of the person telling it. If you aren't keyed in to the relationship between time and ethnicity, you miss the bus.

It isn't just ethnic minorities who ignore Beijing's often schizophrenic regulations. Indeed, while politely paying lip service to the center, provincial and local governments actively resist, ignore, or undermine any unwelcome policy for as long as possible, just like Mao once told them to do. Beijing responds by issuing more detailed regulations, and thus the pattern continues, with the resistance becoming ever more creative. Since most implementation is left to the provinces themselves, Beijing must channel massive resources into enforcing the laws and regulations it really cares about. If the political stakes are high for everyone involved—as with stamping out the quasi-religious Falungong sect—such an enforcement campaign can be remarkably effective. But if there are strong counter-veiling economic reasons for resistance—as with laws concerning intellectual property protection or attempts to curb investment in certain sectors—Beijing's regulations will be followed only for as long as is necessary to provide local officials with political cover.

The inconsistent and contradictory application of laws and regulations causes tremendous problems when it comes to equity and justice. In one village, the family planning policy might be enforced by carrying a heavily pregnant woman down the mountain on a stretcher to abort her baby and forcibly sterilize her; in a village in a neighboring county, the farmers may all have three or four children for which they pay nominal fines. In one province, the underground Catholic bishops may all be languishing in jail; in another, they may be celebrating open-air masses.

While it is the Chinese themselves who are most affected by such contradictions, it also complicates foreign relations and investment. Diplomats who are trying to negotiate with Beijing on anything from human rights to intellectual property protection must constantly weigh its agreements against what they see in the field, its evident enforcement ability, and its apparent intent. With foreign investors, it is somewhat the opposite; they must first make sure that what a locality promises is actually in agreement with Beijing's regulations. Making such determinations is complicated by the fact that central level ministries penetrate vertically into the provinces and localities, but frequently are at odds with each other. So, one ministry might have every intention of enforcing a particular agreement, while another might actively countermand it; likewise, one might promise the moon, while another will refuse to grant a critical license.

The impact of Mao's contradictory policies · even lingers on in China's industry. Mao, of course, set up a system in which all enterprises were owned by the state but in which each province was encouraged to be self-sufficient. Despite considerable industrial consolidation in the three decades since his death, there is still overcapacity in certain industries and little ability to take advantage of economy of scale; twenty-seven regions and municipalities manufacture cars, and there are more than three thousand pharmaceutical companies. Competition between provinces and localities is bitter, and regional protectionism remains a significant problem. When China was negotiating to join the World Trade Organization (WTO) a few years back, Chinese officials joked that first it needed to create a China Trade Organization to ensure fair trade among its own provinces.

A Tradition of Contradiction

Of China's many opposites, the apparent contradiction of an unelected Communist government managing a booming capitalist system is perhaps most glaring—and difficult for outsiders to understand. To be sure, it is not hard to see the benefits of the post-Mao market reforms that created what is officially known as a "socialist market economy." Between 1978 and 2005, the number of

Chinese living below the poverty line fell from 250 million to 23.65 million—even as the population increased by more than 300 million. China is now one of the world's biggest economies, with economic growth averaging 9 percent a year for two decades running. It maintains a huge external trade surplus and holds foreign exchange reserves of more than 1 trillion in U.S. dollars, the highest of any nation. "Never before has the world seen such sustained growth," wrote the Nobel-prize winning economist Joseph Stiglitz. "Never before has there been so much poverty reduction."

But, wonderful as this growth is, it is nonetheless difficult for many of us to see how a Communist government that presides over an economy in which the private sector now accounts for nearly 70 percent of the national economy can still claim to adhere to "Marxism, Leninism, and Mao Zedong Thought." Or, for that matter, how it can profess to represent "the people" when 120 million of these people live on less than a dollar a day, 100 million have no access to medical care, and as many as 400 million don't have running water—but *Forbes* magazine prints an annual list of the nation's four hundred richest people, which now includes ten billionaires.

Even worse, corruption is rampant, with some estimates putting its value at 3 to 5 percent of China's gross domestic product (GDP), and the Communist Party itself appears to be the biggest offender of all. In

2005, the Central Discipline Inspection Commission disciplined 115,000 Party members for corruption and other violations, of whom 24,000 were expelled and 15,000 sent to the court system to be tried and punished. In 2006, 97,000 were punished, with 3,500 cases handed over to prosecutors, among these seven officials at or above the ministerial rank. The vice-mayor of Beijing was removed from his post for corruption and "dissoluteness," which allegedly involved "sex romps" with his many mistresses. (According to the Hong Kong press, one of the romps was filmed and shown to the Party Politburo before its members voted to dismiss him.) The head of the National Bureau of Statistics was also removed, allegedly for managing to divert several million dollars from Shanghai's pension fund to his Shanghainese mistress and their illegitimate child. And, in the highest fall of all, the Party secretary of Shanghai was removed from office for his alleged involvement in a social security fund scandal. The charge that the Party is becoming an organization of crony capitalists who espouse Communist ideology even as they facilitate lucrative business deals for their children and procure foreign passports for their grandchildren appears ever more true.

It is perhaps not surprising that many outsiders look at these contradictions and assume the end is near. "Lurking beneath the dramatic skylines of Shanghai and Beijing is a political crisis—one that's receiving little attention," began a 2002 National Public Radio program on China. "The giant country is stretching itself around two fundamental contradictions of political and economic development. The resulting 'marriage' between Leninism and capitalism has only deepened the contradiction. How can China's communist party survive as it encourages a system of free market liberalization? Our guest tonight says it can't."

But history, in fact, seems to say it can.

The Communist Party is the heir of a rich tradition of contradictions that come from native Daoism, imported Marxist dialectics, and, most recently, Mao's insistence on the primacy of the unity of opposites. It has likewise inherited Mao's conception of Communism—not the former Soviet Union's—which was flexible, rather than fixed. It has a high comfort level when it comes to contradictions and can find ample ideological justification even for something that appears hypocritical to an outsider, like the merger of communism and capitalism. Indeed, despite his profound dislike for capitalism, Mao himself once said, *"Let them go in for capitalism. Society is very complex. If one only goes in for socialism and not for capitalism, isn't that too simple? Wouldn't we then lack the unity of opposites, and be merely one-sided?"*

The Party demonstrated its special affinity for the unity of opposites in 2002, when it decided to allow private capitalists, lawyers, managers in foreign-invested enterprises and others who would be hard to categorize as proletariat to join its ranks. The decision was framed as entirely in keeping with the "innovative spirit" bequeathed to Chinese Communism by both Mao and Deng. It was also suggested, for the benefit of critics, that failing to "keep up with the times" could doom China's Communist Party to the same fate as the Soviet Union's. While this unique solution to what Mao called the principal contradiction between socialism and capitalism did generate some internal Party opposition, it was greeted with equanimity, even pleasure, by many others both inside and outside the Party. (The Chinese people, after all, are also possessed with a healthy respect for the unity of opposites.)

In fact, contrary to what might be expected if the "marriage between Leninism and capitalism" is doomed, Communist Party membership has actually grown in tandem with the unprecedented market liberalization, economic expansion, and personal freedom of recent years. The Party had 60 million members in 1997 and 70 million members in 2005—and 80 percent of the nearly 2.5 million people who joined the Party in 2005 were under the age of thirty-five. This is partly because joining the Party is seen as a smart career move. But it is also because the Communist Party really is increasingly seen as what former president Jiang Zemin called "the vanguard of the

Chinese people and Chinese nation." As long as the Party can continue to lead China forward into a prosperous future, it will survive; neither ideological contradictions nor prosperity will derail it.

JOIN THE PARTY

The increase in Communist Party membership is even more striking when one considers that joining the Party is hardly akin to an American checking a box to become a Democrat, or a Briton filling out a form and paying thirty-six pounds annually to become a Labor Party member. Indeed, to become a member of the Communist Party, you must receive (or solicit) an invitation, write essays, get sponsors, and work very hard just to be accepted on probation. You must then swear fealty with the oath:

> It is my will to join the Communist Party of China, uphold the Party's program, observe the provisions of the Party Constitution, fulfill a Party member's duties, carry out the Party's decisions, strictly observe Party discipline, guard Party secrets, be loyal to the Party, work hard, fight for communism throughout my life, be ready at all times to sacrifice my all for the Party and the people, and never betray the Party.

Assuming you pass your yearlong probation and become a full member, you will likely gain many professional advantages. One Hong Kong study revealed that the income of Communist Party members is 28 percent higher than that of non-members in urban areas. But the hard work doesn't end once you are accepted. On the contrary, you must plan to devote every Friday afternoon of your working life to long, ideological, and reportedly very dull meetings on such topics as "the important thinking of the three represents" and "the eight honors and eight disgraces." (Unless you are unconcerned about promotion; one Party member I know uses this time to get foot massages.) When there's a rectification, you may have to criticize yourself and your friends, and you will be in serious trouble should you violate Party discipline and get caught by someone with no reason to protect you. When the Party eats its own, it does so in true Maoist style, transforming even administrative issues or political differences into charges of moral depravity and launching public smear campaigns that allow the accused no public opportunity for self defense.

Instead, the greatest threat to its continued rule is the ever more extreme wealth gap which dates to Deng Xiaoping's argument that some must get rich first. Deng's pragmatic approach brought China great benefits, but the contradiction between rich and poor is now increasingly seen as excessive and unsustainable. President Hu Jintao has moved to address the gap both with action—such as eliminating the agricultural tax in 2006—and rhetoric, such as his invocation of Mao's early populism and emphasis on *"plain living and hard struggle."* In autumn of 2006, the Communist Party officially endorsed President Hu's call for the creation of a "harmonious socialist society" putting social issues on the same level as economic issues for the first time since Mao. "There are many conflicts and problems affecting social harmony," declared the official statement. "Our party has to be more proactive in recognizing and dissolving these contradictions." As Mao said, it is the opposites in a contradiction that impel things to move and change, and a change in emphasis, at least, is underway.

HU NEEDS MAO?

Deng Xiaoping preserved Mao's reputation for posterity and kept much of his political legacy intact. Deng's successor Jiang Zemin paid requisite, if not ardent, homage to Mao Zedong Thought and in 1993 made a pilgrimage to Mao's hometown to unveil a bronze statue marking the one-hundredth anniversary of the Chairman's birth. (The arrival of the statue, I learned when I visited, pleased Mao and caused three miracles: a mysterious echo appeared on his parents' grave; azaleas bloomed in December; and the sun and the moon aligned themselves in broad daylight.) But China's current leader, Hu Jintao, has been downright effusive in his praise of Chairman Mao. On December 26, 2003—the 110th anniversary of Mao's birth—President Hu led his Politburo colleagues to the Chairman Mao Memorial Hall. They bowed three times before the huge marble Mao statue and then paid respects to the Chairman's embalmed remains. Afterwards, President Hu called Mao "a great Marxist; a great proletarian revolutionary, strategist, and theorist; a great patriot and national hero in modern-day China; and a great man of his generation who led the Chinese people to thoroughly change their destinies and the face of their nation."

In 2004, Hu instructed that a "Red Tour" program be launched in Mao's birthplace of Shaoshan, with the goal of attracting one million Chinese students to visit it during their summer vacation. (That target was exceeded by a million, and Red Tourism to Shaoshan and other sites remains hot.) To celebrate the 2006 Spring Festival, Hu traveled to the old Communist base of Yanan to visit the caves where Mao and other revolutionary leaders once lived. He urged that the "Yanan Spirit" be used as "an important magic weapon for overcoming difficulties and seizing victories" in the process of building a well-off society.

Hu seems to be borrowing the image and words of the young Mao—as yet unblemished by political disaster and personal excess—to revive a spirit of equality and sacrifice that went missing in the era of "to get rich is glorious." This is likely to be an uphill battle, so odds are President Hu will continue channeling Chairman Mao's (younger) ghost.

Dialectics dictates that China will not forever remain a "socialist market economy" ruled by the Communist Party.

One thing destroys another, things emerge, develop and are destroyed, everywhere is like this...Do you believe they can carry on for a million years with the same economics? Have you thought about it? If that were so, we wouldn't need economists, or in any case we could get along with just one textbook, and dialectics would be dead.

But the Party's staying power may be much greater than we anticipate and the contradictions that finally do it in are unlikely to be the ones upon which we outsiders focus.

A CRYSTALLIZATION OF COLLECTIVE WISDOM

Now let's consider some of the ways China's myriad contradictions might impact your business and how you can defend yourself against them, and even turn them to your favor.

- **A Sino-foreign joint venture is a unity of opposites.**

  Mao knew from his experience cooperating with the Nationalist party how difficult it is to join forces to achieve a common goal. *"What is synthesis? You have all witnessed how the two opposites, the [Nationalist Party] and the Communist Party, were synthesized on the mainland. The synthesis took place like this: their armies came, and we devoured them, we ate them bite by bite...One thing eating another, big fish eating little fish. This is synthesis."* Before you agree to form a joint venture with a Chinese company, you must ask yourself, "Who is the big fish and who is the little fish?" If you suspect that your potential partner's ultimate goal is to devour your technology, your capital, or your know-how, then swim away. There are other fish in the sea.

- **MAKE THE COMMUNIST PARTY YOUR ALLY.**

The Communist Party is China's most important business organization; it has ultimate approval over every investment and branches in all state-owned enterprises and 85 percent of private enterprises. Party members are present at the negotiation stage of any major deal. They may come and go at random, be badly dressed, carry no business cards, or have unimportant-sounding titles such as non-executive director. But they have the power and you need to know who they are and what they want. The Party is equally important in the operational phase of an investment, especially if it is a joint venture. If you want to succeed in China, you must understand how the Communist Party works, what it wants, and what it can do for you.

- **USE CONTRADICTIONS TO YOUR ADVANTAGE.**

The Chinese government is a master at using contradictions to its own advantage. It demands to be treated as a developing nation in international trade negotiations but as a major global power at the United Nations. It issues laws and regulations that contain conflicting or opaque clauses and then waits to see what happens before clarifying them. Most Chinese people—be they entrepreneurs or artists—are accustomed to this and understand that the space between two contradictions is called opportunity. But outsiders, especially from the West, grow nervous when operating on vaguely defined legal or contractual grounds. If you can approach China's contradictions with some flexibility, you will broaden opportunities and remove impediments.

- **DON'T GET CAUGHT IN AN ANTAGONISTIC CONTRADICTION.**
  Some companies assume, or are encouraged to believe, that the many gray areas in Chinese law give them license to skirt laws or regulations that are clear. For example, a local government might suggest that a large project which needs central level approval should be broken into two smaller projects that do not need approval. Such arrangements may seem beneficial in the beginning, but they will inevitably come back to haunt you—if the law is clear, you had best follow it.

- **BE AWARE OF REGIONAL STEREOTYPES.**
  When we look at China, we see Chinese people. But, when a Chinese person looks at China, he sees "arrogant" Beijingers, "lily-livered" Shanghainese, "uncultured" Cantonese—and so on. Stereotyping each other is China's national parlor game, nowadays played primarily in Internet chat rooms. These real

and perceived differences make it difficult to transfer Chinese executives. They also translate into discrimination. Migrant workers suffer most, but even professionals from one region who are posted to another will have to overcome negative stereotypes. If the person is a Chinese from outside China—Taiwan, Singapore, Hong Kong, or elsewhere—he will generally be viewed with a mixture of suspicion, envy, and disdain that will take time to conquer. Service-oriented multinationals are also likely to find that they need to aggressively train their Chinese employees to treat other Chinese with the same respect they accord foreigners.

- **CHINA'S REGIONAL DIVERSITY MAKES IT A MARKETING CHALLENGE MORE AKIN TO EUROPE THAN THE UNITED STATES.**

China's varying climates, cuisines, dialects, economic levels and even temperaments must be considered in any marketing strategy. One recent survey found that consumer preference differed markedly not just by age and gender, but by region. The most sought-after appliance in Beijing, for example, was a microwave; in Shanghai digital video recording systems; in Shenyang a refrigerator; and in Chengdu a laptop. Marketers find that advertising must be highly targeted, or at least tested to ensure it doesn't alienate anyone; a commercial that amuses Shang-hainese may enrage Beijingers and leave Cantonese yawning. Even language must be considered—a 2004 survey by China's Ministry of Education reported that more than 40 percent of China's people cannot speak standard Mandarin. While most understand it, they may respond better to advertisements that take account of their own language or dialect.

- **BUSINESS METHODS MUST BE REGIONALLY CALIBRATED.**
  The management skills that serve you well in Beijing simply may not work in Shanghai. Beijingers, for example, may be more sensitive to perceived arrogance, while Shanghainese will be hell bent on making sure they get the same perks as their colleagues. If you work in different cities, it is essential to view them as different cultures and take the time to understand them. Likewise, the investment plums you offer in one city may fail to entice in another. Governments, like people, have very different concerns and priorities which you need to understand to win a deal and make it work.

- **BECOME AN EXPERT IN OPPOSITES.**
  China is both admiring of things foreign and xeno-phobic; convinced of the superiority of Chinese

culture and plagued by a (decreasing) sense of inferiority; and a nation of confident patriots and paranoid nationalists. Your experience will fluctuate with the reigning national sentiment. It will also vary greatly depending on your nationality, race, age, and line of work. (Gender doesn't matter as much.) If you want respect, tell people you're a businessperson; if you want a lower price, tell them you're a writer. Your professional experience will also depend greatly on the reputation of your company and the size of the investment it is making. If you work for a Fortune 100 company that is investing $200 million in Shanghai to build a state-of-the-art plant, you will find the government to be remarkably responsive and accessible; if you are investing $3 million in a widget factory, you will consider yourself lucky if a big city bureaucrat takes your phone call.

- **BE PREPARED TO HEAR ONE THING AND SEE ANOTHER—AND VICE VERSA.**
In 1970, as Mao was contemplating ways to restart a relationship with the United States, he wrote an essay called "People of the World Unite and Defeat U.S. Aggressors and All Their Running Dogs." In it, he declared that *"Nixon's fascist atrocities have kindled the raging flames of the revolutionary mass movement in the*

United States...the Nixon government is beset with troubles internally and externally, with utter chaos at home and extreme isolation abroad." But when he met with Nixon two years later, he told him *"I voted for you during your election"* and in subsequent meetings with Kissinger dismissed the Watergate scandal as *"breaking wind...very meager, yet now such chaos is being kicked up because of it. Anyway, we are not happy about it."* Mao also bluntly suggested to Kissinger that it would be best if both nations sometimes said one thing and did another. *"Actually it would be that sometimes we want to criticize you for a while and you want to criticize us for a while...You say, away with you Communists. We say, away with you imperialists. Sometimes we say things like that. It would not do not to do that."* Official rhetoric and actual policy still sometimes deviate dramatically in times of diplomatic strife and it is important to remember this when reacting. On the other hand, a promise is not always what it seems—in China, as everywhere, actions speak louder than words.

- **REMEMBER THAT THE ABSENCE OF REGULATION IS NOT FREEDOM.**
  The Communist Party has ceded considerable control over the lives of Chinese people over the past three decades, but it has not rejected the principle that it should control whatever it wants; on the contrary, it

understands that giving up some control is the best (and most economical) way to maintain overall control and preserve the one-Party system.

To maintain control while relinquishing it, the Party increasingly relies on its ability to make people police themselves. This was a favorite tactic of Chairman Mao. Indeed, one of his more diabolical leadership strategies was "letting the snakes come out of their holes" by withdrawing from direct leadership or withholding his opinion so he could see what others would do and say. This is essentially how China controls media and Internet content. "Under the strict conditions of the propaganda department, all Chinese people are used to restraining themselves," explained Li Datong, the former editor of *Freezing Point*. "They live under a threat that they haven't articulated to themselves, but which they feel. And this permanent feeling of fear they have turned into a way of life." Do not live and work in fear, but do understand that behind the glitz and growth of contemporary China there remain lines which cannot be crossed. When it comes to political sensitivities, your Chinese colleagues are likely to understand these lines far better than you and it is in your interest—and theirs—to seek their counsel and to err on the side of caution.

- **GO INTO CHINA WITH AN EXIT STRATEGY.**

Most foreign investors expend so much effort entering the China market that they do not consider what will happen when they need to leave. But, the reality is that every investment is ultimately finite and when it comes time to go, you may be asked to pay dearly (for compensation to laid-off workers, disposal or sale of equipment, taxes and miscellaneous fees, public relations, and the like.) Planning ahead will help to mitigate the shock and put you in a better position to negotiate a graceful—and affordable—departure. Should you find yourself doubting the need for an exit plan, remember Mao's warning: *"What indissoluble ties are there in this world? Things may be tied, but in the end they must be severed. There is nothing which cannot be severed...We must take life as our starting-point in discussing the unity of opposites."*

NOTES:

The law of the unity of opposites—in "On the Correct Handling of Contradictions Among the People," February 27, 1957.

Manuscripts lined bookshelves along—in Kissinger, *The White House Years*, p. 1058.

The more books one reads—in Schram, p. 232.

I think our attitude should be—in "Excerpts from a Speech at the Moscow Meeting of Representatives of the Communist and Workers' Parties," November 18, 1957.

with twenty-two existing provinces—in "The Fundamental Problem of Hunanese Reconstruction: The Republic of Hunan," September 3, 1920, in *Road to Power,* Volume I, p. 545.

more harm than good and *stand up for independence*—in "Complete Self-Rule and Semi-Self Rule" October 3, 1920, in *Road to Power,* Volume I, p. 563.

I oppose the 'Great Republic of China'—in "The Fundamental Problem of Hunanese Reconstruction: The Republic of Hunan," September 3, 1920, in *Road to Power,* Volume I, p. 543.

The localities have the right to resist all impracticable—in "Talk at Enlarged Meeting of the Political Bureau," April 1956, in Kau, *Writings of Mao,* Vol. II, p. 69.

Between 1978 and 2005, the number of Chinese living—in "Press officer: Poor population in China fell from 250 million in 1978 to 23.65 million in 2005." Chinese Embassy website.

Never before has the world seen—in "Development in defiance of the Washington consensus" Joseph Stiglitz, *The Guardian,* April 13, 2006.

120 million of these people live on less than a dollar a day, 100 million have no access to medical care, and 400 million don't have running water—in "Health Poverty Quite Serious in China," *People's Daily,* July 14, 2003.

Lurking beneath the dramatic skylines—in On Point, "China's Dot Communism," August 27, 2002.

"Let them go in for capitalism—in Schram, "Talk on questions of philosophy," August 18, 1964, p. 216.

The Party had 60 million members in 1997—in *People's Daily*, March 8, 2006.

It is my will to join the Communist—see "Full Text of the Constitution of the Communist Party of China," www.china.org.ca.

a great Marxist; a great proletarian—in "Hu Jintao Speech at CPC Forum on Mao Zedong's 110th Birth Anniversary," Beijing Xinhua Domestic Service in Chinese, December 26, 2003 (FBIS translation).

In 2004, Hu instructed that a "Red Tour"—in "Following Instruction by Hu, 'Red Tour' To Be Launched in Mao's Birthplace," June 16, 2004 (FBIS translation).

"One thing destroys another, things emerge— in Schram, 227.

What is synthesis? You have—in Schram, p. 224.

The most sought after appliance in Beijing—in survey by UPS.

"I voted for you during your election—in Kissinger, *The White House Years*, p. 1061.

breaking wind...very meager—in Kissinger, *Years of Upheaval*, p. 690.

Actually it would be that sometime—in *Kissinger Transcripts*, p. 88.

Under the strict conditions of the—in "China's media censorship rattling world image," Robert Marquand, *The Christian Science Monitor*, January 24, 2006.

What indissoluble ties are there—as quoted in Schram, p. 224.

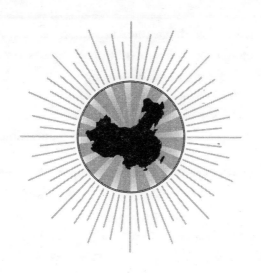

CHAPTER THREE

MAKE FOREIGN THINGS
SERVE CHINA

Make the past serve the present, make foreign things serve China.

We learn foreign things because we want to study and develop Chinese things.

That foreign things should serve China is a key tenet of Mao's teachings—one that remains strong, if more subtly expressed, to this day. This pragmatic attitude to things foreign presents a challenge to many outsiders, who see it as unsavory, but in fact this approach can ultimately benefit you as much as it does China.

Blame History

One of Mao's earliest introductions to the world beyond China came by way of a book written by a scholar who had worked with Westerners and come to admire their technology and know-how but who feared their intentions in China.

> *"I used to cover up the window of my room late at night so that my father would not see the light,"* Mao explained. *"In this way I read a book called 'Words of Warning,' which I liked very much. The author...thought that the weakness of China lay in her lack of Western appliances—railways, telephones, telegraphs, and steamships—and wanted to have them introduced into the country...'Words of Warning' stimulated in me a desire to resume my studies."*

Around the same time that Mao read "Words of Warning" he also secretly perused a pamphlet that prophesied the dismemberment of China by these same foreign countries.

> *I remember even now that this pamphlet opened with the words, 'Alas, China will be subjugated!'...After I read this I felt depressed about the future of my country and began to realize that it was the duty of all people to help save it.*

Mao's belief that it was his duty to save China stayed with him throughout his life—accompanied by a strong ambivalence about the role the outside world should play in this quest.

> *"Foreign languages are truly doors which we must open,"* he wrote to a friend when he was in his early twenties. *"I am now studying a little English every day. If I can keep at it, I will be able to gain some small benefit."*

But, that same year he complained to a different friend that,

> *"Too many people are infatuated with the two words 'going abroad.' There are no fewer than tens of thousands, or even hundreds of thousands, of Chinese who have been abroad. Only very few of them are really good. As for the majority, they are still 'muddled,' still 'unable to make head or tail of it.'"*

Mao studied English sporadically until he was an old man, but he never really learned to speak it, or went to a country where it was actually spoken. Indeed, though he traveled incessantly within China, he ultimately ventured abroad only twice, both times to visit the USSR.

At the same time, Mao's ambivalence to the world outside China never led him to condemn all things foreign. On the contrary, he opposed those who did, pointing out that Marxism was foreign and stating that *"we openly put forward the slogan of learning from foreign countries, learning all their advanced and superior things and continuing to learn them for ever."* Yet he always maintained a deep-rooted suspicion of the intentions of foreign nations, allies and enemies alike, and he insisted that anything foreign be used to serve Chinese interests.

This "serving China" litmus test applied to virtually all of Mao's dealings with the outside world, affecting diplomatic and economic relationships alike. In the 1940s, Mao told an American journalist who interviewed him at the Communist base camp of Yanan that he considered the United States to be *"the most suitable country"* to assist in China's modernization and even wondered if Sears, Roebuck would extend its catalogue business to China!

As it happened, the international situation—and his own visceral hatred of capitalism—prevented Mao from developing any kind of commercial relationship with the

West. *"Why do these countries do business with us,"* he once asked of the United States and Britain, *"and, supposing they might be willing to lend us money on terms of mutual benefit in the future, why would they do so? Because their capitalists want to make money and their bankers want to earn interest to extricate themselves from their own crisis—it is not a matter of helping the Chinese people."*

But Mao had no such compunctions when it came to the USSR. Within weeks of the establishment of the People's Republic, Mao was on a train to Moscow in the hope of turning Soviet support for China's Communist Party into practical assistance in building up his new nation's economy. Mao first explained to Stalin that China needed *"a period of three–five years of peace, which would be used to bring the economy back to pre-war levels"* and then asked directly for economic aid:

> Comrade Mao Zedong: *We would like to decide on the question of Soviet credit to China, that is to draw up a credit agreement for 300,000,000 dollars between the governments of the USSR and China.*

> Comrade Stalin: This can be done. If you would like to formalize this agreement now, we can.

> Comrade Mao Zedong: *Yes, exactly now, as this*
> *would resonate well in China. At the same time it*
> *is necessary to resolve the question of trade...*

Mao went on to request Soviet help in establishing air routes, creating a navy—even in editing the Chinese originals of his own writings. In coming years, more than 10,000 Soviet experts traveled to China to help develop its industry, agriculture, science, arts, culture, education, nuclear technology, and virtually everything else. Thousands of Chinese also traveled to the USSR for advanced training in their respective fields. The USSR provided the model for everything from steel plants to universities. You can still feel the USSR's influence in China's education system, hear its influence in China's symphony orchestras, and see its influence in 1950s architecture.

This "brotherly" economic relationship was serving China well, but Mao was not one to express much appreciation for help that he evidently considered China's due. Instead, he increasingly chafed at what he deemed Moscow's patronizing attitude and in 1958 even complained to an evidently frustrated Khrushchev about the quality of the advice given by some of the Soviet advisers.

> Khrushchev:...But the conditions are unfair
> for us. You can bring complaints about the

follies of our specialists, and we do not have your specialists. Therefore it turns out that only we commit follies.

Mao: *History is to blame for this.*

Khrushchev: And we have to answer for this?

Mao: *You made a revolution first.*

Khrushchev: And we should be blamed for this?

Tense relations between the two Communist giants were further exacerbated by a host of other differences, including Khrushchev's 1959 visit to the United States, which came at a bad time for China (in the midst of the Great Leap famine), and infuriated Mao. In 1960, Moscow recalled all its advisers from China.

The loss of Soviet advice and assistance had a significant psychological and economic impact. Across China, major projects were left half-finished as Soviet advisers tore up blueprints and technical documents and headed back home. Mao's latent suspicion of the intentions of all foreign nations was reinvigorated, and he essentially determined that China would go it alone. When Chinese engineers finally finished a bridge spanning the turbulent Yangtze River at Nanjing in 1968—

a project that Soviet advisors had worked on but deemed impossible—it became a cause for national celebration. (Should you visit Nanjing on business, you will undoubtedly hear about the Great Nanjing Bridge and may even be obliged to go see it.)

In 1964, the Soviet Communist Party sent a letter to China suggesting that they patch things up, return the advisers, hold border talks, and get trade going again. Mao was willing to hold border talks, but the other points no longer interested him.

However, by 1970, Mao had decided that it was impractical to be enemies with two global powers at the same time—so he would reach out to the United States. *"Didn't our ancestors counsel negotiating with faraway countries while fighting with those that are near?"* When the United States-China dialogue opened in 1971, secretly at first, Mao seemed to have shocked even Henry Kissinger, the master practitioner of *realpolitik*, by his willingness to discard ideology in favor of policies that better served Chinese interests. "Mao Zedong," wrote Kissinger, "the father of China's Communist revolution, who had convulsed his people in his effort to achieve doctrinal purity, went to great pains to show that slogans scrawled on every wall in China were meaningless, that in foreign policy national interests overrode ideological differences."

Mao even made a jocular attempt at starting up a

win-lose trade relationship:

> Chairman Mao: *The trade between our two countries at present is very pitiful. It is gradually increasing. You know China is a very poor country. We don't have much. What we have in excess is women.* (laughter)

> Dr. Kissinger: There are no quotas for those or tariffs.

> Chairman Mao: *So if you want them we can give a few of those to you, some tens of thousands.* (laughter)

> Prime Minister Zhou: Of course on a voluntary basis.

> Chairman Mao: *Let them go to your place. They will create disasters. That way you can lessen our burdens.* (laughter)

He also displayed an eagerness to learn "*foreign things.*" "*I don't know much about the United States,*" he told President Nixon. "*I must ask you to send some teachers here, mainly teachers of history and geography.*" On another occasion, he told Kissinger that Chinese needed to learn foreign languages and he would send more people overseas to study.

As it happened, the all-consuming fires of internal politics (in both China and the U.S.) prevented Mao from realizing his scheme to dump excess women on the American market or open up educational exchanges—China's full opening to the outside world would have to wait for his death. But, the combination of admiration, suspicion, and pragmatism through which Mao viewed the outside world survived him and continues to color virtually all of China's significant relationships.

Developing Chinese Things

To be sure, Mao's successors have tempered his often belligerent approach to foreign policy and instead emphasize his concept of "*mutual benefit*" as they assert China's interests. While he was oblivious to international opinion, they are generally solicitous of it. And where Mao in his final years sought economic independence, his successors have staked their political future on economic integration and interdependence. But, the Communist Party has never deviated from Chairman Mao's basic philosophy—that foreign things should be made to serve China.

A PEACEFUL THREAT?

Mao was singularly unconcerned about what outsiders thought of him, in matters small and large. Shortly after liberation, his protocol chief suggested that he follow international custom by wearing a dark suit and black leather shoes to receive foreign ambassadors. *"We Chinese have our own customs,"* Mao replied angrily. *"Why should we follow others?"* He went on to forge his own sartorial path—wearing the simple collarless jacket and pants known outside China as a Mao suit, and sometimes greeting guests in a towel—and his own political path.

China's current leaders generally wear the dark, Western-style suits that Mao rejected—and care correspondingly more about what outsiders think, in matters small and large. In 2006, the government began a campaign to get its citizens to behave in a more civilized manner overseas; it even issued "Chinese Citizens Behavior Guidelines for Outbound Trips" so there would be no ambiguity.

While Beijing is officially dismissive of Western fears of a "China threat," it nonetheless makes efforts to allay them. Initially, it tried to counter arguments that China threatened the West by emphasizing China's desire for a "peaceful rise" to general prosperity. When the word "rise" was singled out as threatening by some U.S. commentators, it was quietly changed to "peaceful development." Most recently, Beijing has floated the idea of the

"China dream" to build a prosperous and revitalized Chinese civilization in a peaceful world.

These scenarios were articulated by Communist Party advisor Zheng Bijian who explains that the "China dream" will differ from the American dream, which involved excessive consumption; the European dream, which included colonization; and the Soviet dream, which was accompanied by an arms race and the export of revolution. (He neglects to mention China's previous dreams of building nuclear weapons and exporting revolution, or its current support of states widely seen as rogues in the international order.) Instead, he stresses that China will make its own way forward in the world and promises that "We will only export computers, not revolution."

When Deng Xiaoping came to power in 1979 and launched the policy of "reform and opening" to the outside world, he made it clear that learning from the outside world to develop China would be the fundamental goal of foreign economic cooperation.

"We must learn to manage the economy by economic means," he explained in echoes of Mao. "If we ourselves don't know about advanced methods of economic management, we should learn from those who do either at home or abroad."

Deng allowed foreign companies to trade with and

invest in China and gave select Chinese companies permission to do the same overseas. But it all took place under carefully managed conditions that included import and export controls, a dual currency system, and a rigorous government approval process. While many outsiders looked at the changing economic policies and assumed that Deng was preparing to abandon the teachings of Karl Marx for those of Adam Smith, he made it abundantly clear that he had no such intentions.

"Foreign investment will doubtless serve as a major supplement in the building of socialism in our country," Deng told a Japanese delegation in 1984. "And as things stand now, that supplement is indispensable. Naturally, some problems will arise in the wake of foreign investment. But its negative impact will be far less significant than the positive use we can make of it to accelerate our development."

In the years since, China has carefully managed foreign investment by sector, region, type, and size and used it to support its own development priorities. Until the late 1990s, it insisted that foreign companies in most sectors form joint ventures with Chinese partners. This ensured that Chinese companies would share in any profits and acquire (at least in theory) foreign management skills. It also served to ease historic anxiety over the prospect of foreigners once again entering China and controlling chunks of its economy.

As trade and investment began to grow—and with it China's GDP and living standards—it became obvious that foreign investment was indeed accelerating China's development. Economic planners then decided that increased competition would encourage faster reform at moribund state-owned enterprises, and China started to allow the establishment of wholly-foreign owned enterprises in many sectors. When the reforms met some resistance from those who were negatively affected by them, the decision was made to accelerate long-running negotiations to join the World Trade Organization. The negotiations were successfully concluded in 2001 after China agreed to a host of market-opening measures that have significantly deepened its economic integration with the outside world.

EXTERNAL PRESSURE POINTS

China does not respond well to outside pressure—a reality that generally takes every new American administration or British prime minister some time to learn. But it nonetheless recognizes the value of such pressure when it is self-inflicted. It was for this reason that Mao held off on attempting to recover the "renegade province" of Taiwan. "*Some of our comrades don't understand the situation,*" he told his doctor. "*They want us to cross the sea and take over Taiwan. I don't agree. Let's leave Taiwan alone. Taiwan keeps the pressure on us. It helps maintain our internal unity. Once the pressure is off, internal disputes might break out.*" He said much the same thing to Kissinger, adding, "*We are in no hurry about Hong Kong either. We don't even touch Macao...Khrushchev has cursed us, saying why is it you don't want even Hong Kong and Macao.*" China's current leaders also make use of outside pressure to maintain unity and further reforms, as with its accession to the WTO after fifteen years of negotiations; its successful bid for the 2008 Olympics; and even its encouragement for overseas stock exchange listings by strong domestic companies.

Success Breeds Ambivalence

The success of China's effort to use foreign trade and investment to develop its economy is undeniable. Between 2001 and 2006, its exports rose from $266 to $969 billion and imports from $243.6 to $792 billion, making it the world's third largest trading nation. Foreign direct investment has also climbed substantially, from roughly $46 billion in 2001 to just over $63 billion in 2006, making China one of the world's top destinations for overseas investment. It is now regularly referred to as an "economic superpower"; some analysts drop the qualifying "economic" and simply call it "the emerging superpower."

But the old ambivalence about the role that foreign countries should play in China's economy lingers on, and has even grown stronger in parallel with the nation's growing economic might. It rose to the surface in 2005 after several years of increasing merger and acquisition (M&A) activity which included the purchase of major stakes in domestic companies by overseas buyers, a sensitive transaction in any nation. Such acquisitions were encouraged by the government in its effort to privatize underperforming state-owned enterprises, but it was perhaps inevitable that they would trigger historic anxieties about foreign control. Critics were galvanized in the spring of 2006 when a ranking former official publicly cautioned "If China lets multinationals' malicious mergers and acquisitions go ahead freely, China can only act as labor in the global supply chain." The official, who was once director of the State Statistics Bureau, warned darkly that acquisitions by foreign companies would cause Chinese brands to disappear, curtail the nation's ability to innovate, and perhaps even lead to foreign monopolization of entire industries.

With the floodgates open, criticism of FDI has spread beyond M&A. As the official English-language newspaper *China Daily* explained in 2006, "The Chinese-language press is asking whether China, having been the world champion in attracting FDI, has, in fact, attracted too much? Is FDI affecting the nation's "economic security" by attempting to take over some largest State-owned enterprises? Is FDI dominating too many industries and forming new monopolies?"

FDI critics charge that China is too dependent on foreign investment (just as it was once too dependent on trade and assistance from the Soviet Union). Exports by foreign-invested enterprises accounted for 58.3 percent of its total exports in 2005 (an increase of 31.2 percent over 2004), while imports and exports by foreign-invested firms together accounted for 58.5 percent of its total foreign trade in 2005. Since its trade has been in surplus for years, Beijing has come under increasing pressure to purchase more American and European-made goods and to allow its currency to appreciate (so Chinese goods will be less competitive). This pressure is considered annoying, particularly because only about half the content of exported goods is produced in China. Aside from complicating diplomatic relationships, the influx of so much cash also makes it harder for the Chinese government to control economic growth, which was 10.7 percent in 2006.

FDI critics also argue that the preferential tax policies given to multinational investors as a means of attracting investment are nowadays both unwarranted and unfair (especially to private Chinese companies who receive neither the tax benefits granted multinationals nor the subsidized bank loans given to state-owned enterprises). Some complain that China's dependency on foreign investment will only be eased if it improves its own research and development capacity but that this effort is hampered by the more than 750 foreign-invested R & D centers, which are said to hire the best researchers and effectively create an internal talent outflow. There are also increasing questions about the levelness of the international playing field since the Chinese oil giant CNOOC was essentially forced to withdraw its bid to acquire the American oil company Unocal in 2005 because of intense political opposition from the U.S. Congress.

These arguments—some of which have merit and some of which are little more than sour grapes—have made an impact. In 2006, China delayed several high-profile acquisitions of domestic companies by overseas investors. It also passed a number of regulations intended to slow investment in certain sectors and allay fears that it is the foreigners who are using China instead of the other way around. These include limits on foreign investment in real estate; a moratorium on foreign acquisitions of Chinese brokerages; new regulations governing M&A, which now requires central government approval if the acquisition involves "economic security" or a "key Chinese brand"; and approval of a draft version of an anti-monopoly law that is widely believed to be aimed at preventing multinationals from dominating their respective industries. In 2007, the

National People's Congress passed a law that will unify the corporate income tax for foreign and domestic companies at a rate of 25 percent when it comes into effect in 2008. (Under longstanding regulations designed to encourage foreign investment, domestic companies have been officially taxed at 33 percent and foreign-invested enterprises at 15 percent, although the effective rates are respectively closer to 23 percent and 11 percent.)

The international media have reported widely on China's "new ambivalence" to foreign investment and noted that it "marks an important shift in Chinese thinking, with economic and political impact." But the ambivalence is old, rather than new, and the shift in thinking is only partial—China is merely reconsidering the best way to continue using foreign things to serve its developmental goals. Deng Xiaoping believed that foreign investment was an indispensable supplement to building socialism, but more than two decades —and many hundreds of billions of dollars—later his successors are beginning to wonder if there are other paths to achieving their goals.

China is not turning its back on foreign investment— even the critics know it is an essential element in the nation's continued growth and stability. As President Hu Jintao told a gathering of corporate executives during his 2006 U.S. visit, "We welcome more American businesses to China to make investment and transfer their technologies." But—as Hu's word choice indicates—China is getting pickier. In coming years, the central government will try to reduce the nation's dependence on foreign investment and trade and focus more on "sustainable growth" generated by domestic consumption. It will push for higher value, high-tech exports and the creation of a knowledge-led, innovation-oriented economy. It will aim to upgrade existing industries rather than expand them and strive to develop the services sector. It will focus on building up Chinese brands, developing Chinese intellectual property, and helping Chinese companies "go global." These aspirations are no secret—many of them are outlined in the five-year plan for economic and social development that began in 2006 and runs until 2010.

Nor, for that matter, is it any secret that the fundamental reason multinational corporations are allowed to invest in China is because their presence enables Chinese companies to learn from them—if you are investing in China, you are being used. Most Westerners don't like to hear this—we prefer to speak about the lofty benefits of free trade and globalization. But national interest is a legitimate stance, largely devoid of the hypocrisy that accompanies espousals of the virtues of free trade, and has the great advantage of letting you know where you stand. Most multinational executives are well aware that their success in China correlates to their perceived usefulness and take great pains to emphasize their ability to help China through the transfer of technology, management skills, business know-how, and the like. They also understand that in the process of helping China to achieve its goals, they may well be helping to create competitors who will one day confront them not only in China, but in markets around the world. But they invest anyway—and with good reason.

As Mao once said, quoting Confucius, *"If a thing comes to me, and I give nothing in return, that is contrary to propriety."* China may use foreign companies to further its own goals, but it still respects propriety. This was explained clearly by Rick Wagoner, the CEO of General Motors, when a reporter asked if he feared that China would one day use the knowledge it had gained from working with companies like GM to become a competitor. "To be completely fair about it," Wagoner replied, "China has let us come in at an early stage. Japan did not; Korea did not. They basically closed the markets and said we're having only local companies, and they set about policies to help those companies export with huge subsidies. And so here we are, forty or fifty years later, and say, 'That wasn't a very good deal for U.S.-based manufacturers.' China, to their credit, at least is letting us get in to play, to develop our brands, our capabilities. We expect to continue to be a big player over there."

Indeed, in return for the capital, the technology and the know-how, China has given foreign companies the chance to enter the China market and achieve their own evolving goals. It has become, for corporations large and small, a source of affordable labor and raw materials, an export platform, a vast and important market, and a research and development laboratory. And, after many years of being what was generally known as a "strategic investment," it has also finally become a source of profits; in the first half of 2006, corporate profits for U.S. companies in China exceeded $2 billion in U.S. dollars, a 50 percent increase over the same period in 2005. Indeed, 81 percent of the companies who responded to a 2006 U.S.-China Business Council survey reported that their China businesses were profitable and 97 percent were at least somewhat optimistic about their business prospects for the next five years. A 2006 European Chamber of Commerce survey revealed that 61 percent of respondents expected to be profitable while 86 percent were optimistic about doing business in China.

Investing in China is not without risk—Mao made his comments about respecting propriety in a discussion about abandoning the Communist base camp of Yanan to the Nationalist Army under Chiang Kai-shek. *"Chiang,"* Mao said, *"thinks when he has seized the devils' lair, he will win. In fact he will lose everything...We will give Chiang Yanan. He will give us China."* This, in fact, is exactly what happened. Foreign investors must make sure that they don't end up like Chiang Kai-shek, gaining short-term market share and other advantages in China only to lose the global market to a Chinese competitor. The best way to do this is to align your company with government objectives, make yourself useful, and constantly innovate and improve so that you are always two steps ahead of your competitors. That way they will need to keep *"learning all [your] advanced and superior things and continuing to learn them for ever."*

A CRYSTALLIZATION OF COLLECTIVE WISDOM

Now let's consider some of the ways that you can be useful to China—and ensure that your usefulness benefits you, too.

- **BE A REALIST, NOT A MYTHOLOGIST.**
  The myth of the China market dominated late nineteenth and early twentieth century dreams of China and was resurrected when the nation reopened for business in 1979. There are nowadays

few people with experience in China who speak of its market in mythological terms but there is still a widespread sense that "we can't afford not to be there." This may be true, but you still need a sound reason for investing, a good business plan, a realistic sense of the market size for your product, and a brutally honest understanding of the innumerable challenges and problems you will encounter.

- **RECOGNIZE THAT FDI IS NO LONGER KING.**

The days of attracting foreign investment by giving up large parts of China's economy have passed. Provinces and localities remain eager to entice investment, but the central government has a trillion dollars in the bank and is harder to impress; just bringing in money is no longer enough. This makes it all the more crucial to understand what the government wants from foreign investors, at both the central and local levels, and to align yourself with its goals. Look at the five-year plan, the list of "pillar industries," the foreign investment catalogue (which tells whether a particular type of foreign investment project is "encouraged, restricted, or prohibited") and the regional catalogue (which lists encouraged projects for central and western China), talk to as many people as you can, analyze the importance of government support to your project, and, again, be a realist.

- **HELP OTHERS ACHIEVE THEIR GOALS.**

China is an extraordinarily ambitious nation full of equally ambitious people. Everyone you work with has a goal—the government at various levels, your partners, your employees, your customers. If you can help these different entities and individuals to achieve their goals, you will achieve your own faster.

- **HELP CHINA "GO GLOBAL."**

One of Beijing's biggest—and most daunting—goals is to see Chinese manufacturers join the ranks of the world's leading companies. The fastest way to do this is to partner with, or acquire outright, a major foreign brand. The 2005 purchase of IBM's personal computer unit by the Chinese computer maker Lenovo is a relatively successful example of this strategy. But the 2003 majority share joint venture formed by China's TCL Multimedia, the world's largest television maker, with France's Thomson Group was forced into layoffs and a massive restructuring of its European business in 2006. An attempt by Haier, China's top appliance maker, to purchase the venerable American company Maytag failed, as did CNOOC's effort to buy Unocal. Chinese companies, in other words, need help if they are to become global players—the same kind of help that foreign companies need when they go to China. Any assistance you give in supporting the "go global" strategy—advice on managing a merger, understanding local culture, working with the government in your home country—will earn you points.

- **HELP BUILD CHINESE BRANDS.**
Building Chinese brands is an integral part of the "go global" strategy. Only six Chinese brands made the 2006 list of the world's five hundred "most influential brands" (Haier, Lenovo, CCTV, Chang Hong, China Mobile and CREC). When Chinese companies look and act more like global corporations, it will take the pressure off multinationals in China and create a better operating environment for everyone. Since it is going to happen sooner or later, you may as well support the effort (and benefit from your support).

- **TRANSFER SOFT SKILLS.**
China may be cash flush and increasingly choosy when it comes to technology, but it is still in great need of the soft skills—management, innovation, creativity, and leadership—needed to build and run a world-class company. This was one of the original goals of opening and reform and it remains important, especially if Chinese companies are going to succeed with overseas listings, mergers, and acquisitions.

- **BE PREPARED TO DEAL WITH ECONOMIC NATIONALISM IN CHINA.**

  Economic nationalism will ebb and surge, but never disappear. Given the high level of government involvement in the economy, virtually anything can be turned into an issue of national economic security. Nationalist attacks may crop up on the Internet, be sparked by an acquisition attempt, or even by strong sales figures that indicate your business is simply doing too well in China. It may happen that Chinese companies who are normally fierce competitors will join together to fight against you, the foreign "threat." This means that you must proactively plan to counter any nationalist attacks by articulating—to the government, the media, and the public—the many ways in which your business is serving China, and by ensuring that you have adequate government backing.

- **PRACTICE WHAT YOU PREACH.**

  Economic nationalism is not specific to China. The politicized derailing of CNOOC's bid to purchase Unocal in 2005 stunned many Chinese officials, economists and international business people who have for years been hearing the United States preach the benefits of open markets and free trade. In the aftermath of the failed deal, think tanks around the nation were filled with academics trying to understand what went wrong. The impact of this sort of hypocrisy—warning China against "a resurgence of economic nationalism," as the top U.S. trade official did in 2006, while practicing it oneself—should not be underestimated.

- **BE PREPARED TO DEAL WITH CRITICISM AT HOME.** Acknowledging that you are being used to support the Chinese government's goals—and know it—will gain you few points back home. You must therefore be prepared to cogently articulate your reasons for investing in China, and the ways in which your investment will benefit both your shareholders and the Chinese people. Google learned this the hard way when it launched a Chinese language search engine and, like all search engines in China, followed regulations that oblige it to self-censor results. The company was lambasted for "aiding the repression of freedom of information and expression in China" and accused of collaborating with evil itself. The Chinese government is not evil itself and Google does more good than harm by operating in China. Access to censored information is significantly better than no access—especially when the censorship is openly acknowledged—and Google should have launched a more vigorous self defense.

- **HELP CHINA INNOVATE.**

  China's leaders hope to see their nation become a major innovator of new products, technologies, and services. To this end, they have tripled R & D spending over the past decade and President Hu has declared that "independent innovation" is the "core of national competitiveness." But, the dearth of intellectual property protection, the surfeit of government control, and the lack of a genuine peer review system make significant innovation a challenge. You can support efforts to innovate by establishing venture capital funds to invest in Chinese companies doing innovative research; creating research partnerships to work on new technologies together with Chinese entities; contributing to innovative government efforts (like Microsoft's work with the Ministry of Information Industry to help eliminate the urban-rural digital divide or Caterpillar's agreement to help develop China's remanufacturing industry); or participating in innovative new industries emphasized by the government, including biotechnology, nanotechnology, and renewable energy.

- **GET INVOLVED IN THE CREATION OF NEW TECHNOLOGICAL STANDARDS.**

  China has become one of the world's biggest users and producers of technology products. It will have an estimated 520 million cell phone users by the end of 2007 and its high-tech exports have increased from just over $35 billion in 2000 to $218.25 in 2005, or 28.6 percent of overall exports (although many of these come from foreign-invested enterprises). Just as it doesn't want to be factory floor to the world, neither does it want to have technology standards from other nations imposed upon it. Recognizing that technology standards are crucial to their success, many affected companies have invested considerable effort and money in helping China as it develops its own standards.

• HELP CHINESE CULTURE GO GLOBAL.
China's trade is in surplus with the outside world, but its culture is in deep deficit. Hu Jintao is the first top Chinese leader since Mao who has neither studied nor worked abroad. (Deng Xiaoping worked and studied in France and Jiang Zemin did the same in the USSR.) Like Mao, he is said to be deeply rooted in Chinese culture and eager to remedy this galling deficit. To this end, China has established 140 "Confucius Institutes" around the world to promote the learning of Chinese language and culture (a number expected to reach five-hundred by 2010) and is actively promoting cultural exchanges. It will look kindly on any assistance in its effort to bring Chinese culture—language, arts,

books, movies, music and more—to the outside world.

• **YOU ARE EXPECTED TO SERVE CHINA PERSONALLY, TOO.**

A stranger once boarded the Beijing elevator in which I rode with my family, admired my children, glanced at me, and then said to my husband, who is Chinese, "Now that's using foreign things to serve China!" On another occasion, a market vendor called my husband a traitor because he helped me bargain for a lower price. This perception that you are in China to be used—and should therefore pay more for the same item than a Chinese person, help virtual strangers get visas to your home country, be an English teacher to all and sundry, lend money to passing acquaintances on preferential terms, and bear children for the motherland—gets old fast. Your best response is to learn to smile when you want to shout, and to say no without guilt.

• **YOU AREN'T AS USEFUL (OR INTERESTING) AS YOU USED TO BE.**

Foreigners are a dime a dozen in Beijing and Shanghai, and many Chinese have a more sophisticated understanding of the limits to your power and wealth—and may well have more of both than you ever will. This means that awkward requests and absurd assumptions of the sort mentioned above are fewer, but it also means that you will have to work harder to impress. Just as money is no longer enough, neither is a foreign face—instead you need real skill, knowledge, and experience. Fluent Chinese is also likely to become increasingly important as more Chinese take pride in speaking their own language, rather than English.

- **PREPARE FOR THE PROBLEMS OF BEING USEFUL.**
One of the drawbacks of being useful is that there will always be individuals and entities who try to take extra advantage of your usefulness. A joint venture partner might steal your technology and set up a competing factory. A potential partner or customer might glean as much technical information as possible during negotiations and then nix the deal and use the information. A government entity might suddenly demand that you pay local managers the same salary as expatriate managers—but deposit the salary differential into a social welfare fund. If multinationals in your industry seem to be doing well, regulations may be passed to limit the profits you can earn. Patent protection applications may languish until they expire, thereby allowing Chinese companies to legally produce whatever it was you were trying to protect. Imagine any similar scenario and it has probably happened—so always be on your guard.

- **PREPARE FOR TROUBLE IF YOUR USEFULNESS DIMINISHES.**

  You are less useful if you fight the Chinese government. (The United States waited years to file an intellectual property dispute against China at the WTO in part because many American companies did not support it, fearing that by publicly taking on the Chinese government they might ultimately lose more than they gained.)—You are also less useful if you go to court to settle a dispute; lay off workers; close down your operations; or dominate your industry. This does not mean that all of these things cannot be done—but it does mean that you had better be sure that your usefulness in other areas will compensate and that you have a strong relationship with the officials who oversee your industry.

- **STRIKE WHILE THE IRON IS STILL HOT.**

  China's attitude toward foreign investors is evolving. However, for the foreseeable future, local governments will remain eager to attract overseas investment and go to great lengths to support it. M&A activity involving foreign investors has presented more political challenges than expected, but Beijing still officially supports (and needs) it. Economic nationalism may make high-profile—or poorly managed—deals more challenging, but the majority of investments will not be affected.

NOTES:

Make the past serve the present—in *Chinese Literature* 1979, p. 103.

We learn foreign things because—in "Chairman Mao's Talk to Music Workers," August 24, 1956.

I used to cover up the window of—in Snow, p. 133–4.

I remember even now that this—in Snow, p. 136.

Foreign languages are truly doors—in "Letter to Li Jinxi" (1920) *Road to Power* Volume I, p. 518.

Too many people are infatuated—in "Letter to Zhou Shizhao" (1920), in *Road to Power,* p. 504–5.

we openly put forward the slogan—in Schram, p. 82.

the most suitable country—in Short, p. 399.

Why do these countries do business with us—"The People's Democratic Dictatorship," June 30, 1949.

a period of three–five years of peace and Comrade Mao Zedong: *We would like to*—in "Conversation between Stalin and Mao," Moscow, December 16, 1949 (from Cold War International History Project, Smithsonian Institution).

Khrushchev:...But the conditions are unfair for us—in "The Khrushchev-Mao Conversations," July 31–August 3, 1958 and October 2, 1959.

Didn't our ancestors counsel negotiating—in Li Zhisui, *The Private Life of Chairman Mao,* p. 514.

Chairman Mao: The trade between our two countries at present—in *Kissinger Transcripts*, p. 93.

I don't know much about the—in *Kissinger Transcripts*, p. 65.

We Chinese have our own customs—in Li Zhisui, p. 121.

We will only export computers—in Zheng Bijian, "Ten Views on China's Development Road and Peaceful Rise and Sino-European Relations," China Reform Forum, December 15, 2005.

We must learn to manage the economy by economic—in "Conference on Sino-U.S. Educational Exchange," Speech by Yale University President Levin, Nov. 10, 2003.

Foreign investment will doubtless serve—in "Excerpt from a talk with the Japanese delegation to the second session of the Council of Sino-Japanese Non-Governmental Persons," June 30, 1984, quoted in http://english.peopledaily.com.cn/dengxp/vol3/text/c1220.html Deng Xiaoping.

Some of our comrades don't—in Li Zhisui, p. 262.

If China lets multinationals' malicious mergers—in Dai Yan, "Foreign takeover controversial," *China Daily*, April 11, 2006.

The Chinese-language press is asking—in "FDI quality under the microscope," *China Daily*, September 4, 2006.

marks an important shift in Chinese thinking—in Clay Chandler, "China snubs foreign investment," *Fortune*, October 3, 2006.

We welcome more American businesses to China—in "Remarks by Chinese President Hu Jintao to the U.S.-China Business Council, The U.S.-Chamber of Commerce, and The National Committee on U.S.-China Relations," April 20, 2006. (Transcript by Federal News Service.)

If a thing comes to me—in Short, p. 407.

To be completely fair about it—in "Reviving General Motors," Online News Hour with Paul Solman, April 20, 2006, pbs.org.

And, after many years of being what was generally—figure from U.S. Bureau of Economic Analysis as reported in Wiseman, Paul. U.S. Companies profits take off in China. *USA Today*, October 25, 2006.

"Chiang," Mao said, *"thinks when he has . . ."*—in Short, p. 407.

a resurgence of economic nationalism—in "U.S. warns China over rise of 'economic nationalism,'" *Taipei Times*, August 30, 2006.

CHAPTER FOUR

MASTER WHAT YOU DO NOT KNOW

We shall have to master what we do not know...We must acknowledge our ignorance, and not pretend to know what we do not know.

C hina is so vast, diverse, and fast-changing that even Mao felt he didn't understand it enough. The method he used to deepen his understanding is one from which we can all benefit: investigation.

Mastering China

Mao Zedong was by his own account almost comically adrift in his youth. He knew that he wanted to be educated and fought his uneducated father hard for this privilege. He also knew that he wanted to help save China. But he had no idea what sort of education would best further this rather nebulous goal. With no adult to whom he could turn for guidance, he searched for ideas by reading newspaper advertisements. As he explained to Edgar Snow:

> *I had no special standard for judging schools; I did not know exactly what I wanted to do. An advertisement for a police school caught my eye and I registered for entrance to it. Before I was examined, however, I read an advertisement of a soap-making "school." It told of the great social benefits of soap making...I decided to become a soap maker...Meanwhile a friend of mine had become a law student and he urged me to enter his school...Fate again intervened in the form of an advertisement for a commercial school. Another*

friend counseled me that the country was in eco-
nomic war, and that what was most needed were
economists who could build up the nation's econ-
omy. His argument prevailed and I spent another
dollar to register in this commercial middle school.

Mao kept reading ads while waiting for school to start
and soon switched to another commercial school that
promised even more. He attended for a month, but since
most of the classes were in English and he was familiar
with little more than the alphabet, he dropped out, ultimately enrolling in—and matriculating from—a teacher
training school. Several of Mao's classmates left China
for a work-study program in France but, though Mao
helped organize the movement, he did not join it
because "...*I did not want to go to Europe. I felt that I did
not know enough about my own country, and that my time
could be more profitably spent in China.*"

Eventually he made his way to Beijing, where he
found a job at the Peking University library with help
from his former ethics teacher Yang Changji and began
trying to master the subject that would forever be clos-
est to his heart: China.

Peking University in 1918 was a hotbed of intellec-
tual ferment; indeed, the librarian who hired Mao was
Li Dachao, who would in 1921 become a founder of the
Communist Party of China. Mao used his position to

learn as much as he could not just from the books and newspapers that surrounded him, but from the intellectuals who came to read them. However, this wasn't as easy as it sounds.

> *My office was so low that people avoided me. One of my tasks was to register the names of people who came to read newspapers, but to most of them I didn't exist as a human being. Among those who came to read I recognized the names of famous leaders of the renaissance movement, men...in whom I was intensely interested. I tried to begin conversations with them on political and cultural subjects, but they were very busy men. They had no time to listen to an assistant librarian speaking southern dialect.*

But Mao didn't give up. Instead, he joined university study societies, took classes, and continued trying to meet people who would take the time to discuss important matters with an assistant librarian who spoke southern dialect. One woman who did was Yang Kaihui, his esteemed teacher's daughter, whom he married in 1920.

Mao also became a Marxist in 1920 and the following year journeyed to Shanghai for the founding of the Communist Party. But the way ahead was still not clear to him.

Originally I was a feudalist and an advocate of bourgeois democracy. When I joined the Communist Party I knew that we must make revolution, but against what? And how would we go about it? Of course we had to make revolution against imperialism and the old society. I did not quite understand what sort of thing imperialism was, still less did I understand how we could make revolution against it. None of the stuff I had learned in thirteen years was any good for making revolution.

Mao eventually mastered revolution through practice, hard work, and considerable trial and error. But once he was comfortable as a revolutionary, he realized that his position at the head of the Communist Party would be secure only if he were able to make his own theoretical contributions to Marxism, as Lenin and Stalin had done. So, in the mid-1930s, he sequestered himself in his cave at the Communist base camp and immersed himself in tomes of philosophy and economics.

"Mao was an ardent student of philosophy," recalled Edgar Snow. "Once when I was having nightly interviews with him on Communist history, a visitor brought him several new books on philosophy, and Mao asked me to postpone our engagements. He consumed those books in three or four nights of intensive reading, during which he seemed oblivious to everything else."

Mastering theory was not easy for Mao—he was at a disadvantage compared to those who had studied in the USSR—so he got help from a returned student named Chen Boda who was fluent in Russian. He put his theories to paper and in 1937 some of his supporters compiled and published a collection of his essays for the first time. His theoretical writings—*"made up of the universal truth of Marxism-Leninism combined with the concrete reality of China"*—would over time cement his leadership and earn him a place in the Communist canon.

You Must Investigate!

Mastering what you do not know is one of the most difficult aspects of working with China; indeed, if you are new to China—or if China has changed and you have not—it can be a challenge simply to know what you do not know. The first step in the process is to acknowledge your own ignorance—this is hard for many people, especially seasoned executives, diplomats or journalists who think they've seen it all. But if Mao could admit that he didn't know enough about China then the rest of us should be able to do the same. Having done this, we can begin to better understand it by using Mao's favorite method: investigation.

> *You can't solve a problem? Well, get down and investigate the present facts and its past history!*

> *When you have investigated the problem thoroughly, you will know how to solve it. Conclusions invariably come after investigation, and not before. Only a blockhead cudgels his brains on his own, or together with a group, to "find a solution" or "evolve an idea" without making any investigation. It must be stressed that this cannot possibly lead to any effective solution or any good idea.*

Mao's emphasis on investigation again played to his own strengths. As much as he loved learning, it seems to have been hard for him to actually sit down and engage in directed study, especially if it had no immediately practical application. In 1920 he wrote to a friend that he wished he could *"use the X-ray method"* to study many fields, adding, *"I would very much like to study philology, linguistics, and Buddhism, but I have neither the books nor the leisure to study them, so I slack off and procrastinate, and am reduced to saying: "If I fail to study today, there is always tomorrow."*

But investigating China's "actual situation" was something at which he excelled. He believed ardently in the importance of "physical culture" and loved to roam through the countryside meeting ordinary people. As a student, he and a friend spent one summer tramping through five counties of Hunan *"without using a single copper. The peasants fed us and gave us a place to sleep; wherever we went we were kindly treated and welcomed.*" He was inquisitive and analytical, a good listener and a good writer; in his twenties he had aspired to journalism, as well as teaching, and even wrote that "*Most likely, my future livelihood will depend on the salaries from these two jobs.*"

Mao conducted three major investigations while working in the countryside during the second half of the 1920s. The first, which he intended to help him better understand China's social classes, was a month long investigation in his home province of Hunan that dramatically altered his vision of the path that China's Communist revolution should take. The excitement he felt at his discoveries is conveyed in his twenty-thousand-word "Report on an Investigation of the Peasant Movement in Hunan," which also includes some of his most compelling writing.

The report is considered seminal because of Mao's passionate argument that the Party should align itself with the peasants and because of his defense of the violent methods the peasant associations sometimes used. "*A revolution is not a dinner party,*" Mao famously opined, "*or writing an essay, or painting a picture, or doing embroidery; it cannot be so refined, so leisurely and gentle, so temperate, kind, courteous, restrained and magnanimous. A revolution is an insurrection, an act of violence by which one class overthrows another...To right a*

*wrong, it is necessary to exceed the proper limits; the wrong
cannot be righted without doing so."*

Mao cared a great deal about his investigative work.
Thinking that the Hunan report had been lost he
wrote, *"I am not too concerned when I lose things, but los-
ing these investigations caused me pain. For an eternity I
can never forget them."* He produced another rural
investigation at the remote Communist base of Jing-
gangshan in 1928 and a third in 1930, "Report from
Xunwu." The second investigation was, in fact, lost and
the Xunwu investigation was lost for a time and then
recovered, causing Mao great joy—and if you read it,
you'll understand why. The eighty-thousand-word
report on commerce and land relationships is so metic-
ulously researched that you feel as if you are trawling
the markets of a rural county town and chatting with its
merchants right alongside Mao.

Mao's goal in conducting the Xunwu investigation
was to master two subjects in which he considered himself weak. *"I still did not completely understand the problem
of China's rich peasants. At the same time, in the area of commerce, I was a complete outsider. Because of this I pursued this
investigation with great energy."*

In fact, Mao was not a complete outsider to commerce and his interest in the subject shines through.
He noted, for example, that Xunwu had thirty bean
curd stores, but wondered why a city of three thousand

people would need so many. So, he investigated further and discovered that nine out of ten meals included tofu, which was considered cheap and convenient. He then delved into the production process, the cost of the ingredients, and the source of the profits—which came from pigs raised on the leftover soybean residue, rather than the sale of the tofu itself. (Pigs were also the main source of profit for boarding houses, which raised the animals on table scraps.) He concludes by commenting that tofu production is *"learned easily, mastered with difficulty."*

MAO ZEDONG, ENTREPRENEUR

Mao Zedong is not generally thought of as a businessperson, but in his youth he was a successful entrepreneur. His business—The Cultural Book Society—was a non-profit intended to help establish a new culture in his native Hunan by making available important Chinese and foreign books. Mao rented space for the society's headquarters from Yale University's Yale-in-China program (perhaps another historic factor contributing to Yale's strong relationship with China). The Society followed what we might call a Maoist business model. As Mao explained it:

The Cultural Book Society was initiated by a few of us who understand and trust each other completely.

The capital invested, no matter who the investor, can never be withdrawn, and there will never be any dividends. This Book Society will forever be jointly owned by the investors. If it does well, if the capital reaches hundreds of millions, we will not consider it a source of private gains. If it fails and not a penny is left from the venture, we will not blame one another. We will be content to know that on this earth, in the city of Changsha, there was once a "collectively owned" Book Society.

The Society, in fact, did do well and soon had branches in seven counties, a long list of available titles, and profits of over $4,000 Chinese dollars.

Mao approaches every subject he discusses with the same compulsive thoroughness. In addition to listing the names of the thirteen largest general stores, he attaches a *"brief list"* of the 131 *"foreign goods"* they stock, with asterisks to indicate bestselling items such as indigo, nails, flashlights, and tooth powder. His discussion of Xunwu's eight barber shops includes a history of their tools (Western scissors were introduced in 1912 and plastic combs in 1927) and the popularity of different haircuts (shaved heads were "out," "American style" was "in"). He also explains that barbers earned good money but never got rich because their social position was too low to marry, so they spent all their earnings on whoring and gambling. *"Eight of ten barbers do not have wives, but they do not feel miserable at all. They are quite content to frequent brothels.*" The thirty to forty brothels they frequented were staffed by a *"hard-bitten lot of prostitutes"* who mainly came from the town of Sanbiao, which was known for its pretty women. Their main clientele was the sons of landed gentry who enrolled in *"diploma mills."* *"The young masters break away from the warmth of their families when they go to town to study; so they feel quite lonely and leave a lot of footprints leading to brothels."*

Mao was so passionate about investigation that he wanted to share not only its results, but also its methodology. So at the same time he compiled "Report from Xunwu" he also penned an essay on the work of investigation which was published under the title "Oppose Bookism" and begins with the oft-cited phrase, *"no investigation, no right to speak."*

> *"Unless you have investigated a problem, you will be deprived of the right to speak on it,"* Mao explained. *"When you have not probed into a problem, into the present facts and its past history, and know nothing of its essentials, whatever you say about it will undoubtedly be nonsense. Talking nonsense solves no problems...*
> *It won' t do!*
> *It won't do!*
> *You must investigate!*
> *You must not talk nonsense!"*

This sound—if slightly manic—advice was addressed to Communist Party cadres but would be wisely followed by anyone working in or with China. (And this advice could have prevented much tragedy had Mao followed it himself and learned earlier, for instance, that the steel produced in the Great Leap Forward was useless and that diverting resources to its production was leading to the hunger that eventually became famine.)

DON'T SPOUT

Mao believed that there are *"many people who the moment they alight from the official carriage: make a hullabaloo, spout opinions, criticize this and condemn that."* It was in reaction to such people that he created his *"no investigation, no right to speak"* formulation.

Today there are still many people who alight from their airborne carriages and begin to spout opinions on China with only cursory investigation. Depending on to whom you are speaking and depending on the day, China is an economic miracle, the world's biggest market, an unstoppable juggernaut, a future superpower. Or, its market is a myth, its economy a mirage, its banking system a ticking time bomb, and the nation itself a house of cards on the brink of collapse. Some amateur analyses still equate population with market while others focus on huge categories of people like the "emerging middle class" of "30 million to 200 million" or the "affluent nouveau riche" who are experiencing an "enjoy now" phase of consumption.

Such statistics are little more than propaganda and are part of the reason that many companies fail to accurately gauge the real market for their products or services. While Mao was no slouch when it came to propaganda, it is hard to imagine him writing a glossy brochure about "six hundred million disgruntled peasants" experiencing a "rebel now" phase of poverty to convince his colleagues that their revolutionary marketing strategy should be extended to the countryside. *"For such views or criticisms, which are not based on thorough investigation, are nothing but ignorant twaddle."*

Inquire into Everything

If you are a novice—to investigation, China, or both—you should *"Probe deeply. Anyone new to investigation work should make one or two thorough investigations in order to gain full knowledge of a particular place...or a particular problem...Deep probing into a particular place or problem will make future investigation of other places or problems easier."*

Probing deeply means never simply accepting an answer—thirty tofu stores—but always taking the time to understand it. Foreign companies, for example, will sometimes do a market entry survey that counts national competitors but neglects local ones. Yet China still has many local companies with significant market shares in their home territories. It also has a tradition of backyard industry—just think of the Great Leap Forward—which can present unanticipated competition. A frustrated executive once told me that his company had made this mistake and subsequently discovered that many thousands of people produced its product—light bulbs—in their backyards. Some were farmers who made bulbs after the harvest; others were enterprising folk who watched light bulb prices like commodities and produced them whenever the price rose.

Even if an investigation accurately assesses market size, it may neglect underlying factors that could make or break your business. The market for a particular product may, for example, be highly fragmented—if you are selling gypsum or paint for new homes, but most farmers build their own, how will you reach them to sell your product? Likewise, purchasing patterns may be driven by something other than quality and cost. You may have the best product and the best price, but if your competitor is willing to extend credit while you want cash, you could lose out anyway. Or you could find yourself in a similar scenario—best product, best price—but lose out because your competitors are paying kickbacks that your investigation did not uncover.

Most companies that undertake investigative work in China hire specialists to do it for them. But Mao strongly believed that a successful investigation requires personal participation. *"Everyone with responsibility for giving leadership...must personally undertake investigation into the specific social and economic conditions and not merely rely on reading reports. For investigation and reading reports are two entirely different things."*

It is clearly not possible for executives to personally participate in all investigations, but given the importance and cost to a corporation of due diligence, market research, IPR protection, and strategic advice provided by consulting companies, it would seem that the higher the level of personal involvement, the better the likelihood of a successful outcome and implementation. Also, language is no excuse; Mao didn't understand the Xunwu dialect and had to do much of his work through interpreters. He was also presumably just as busy as most executives, and he did not have at his disposal an army of secretaries, MBAs, and consultants to assist him. Although he eventually took charge of a real army—whose members he required to do investigative work—he conducted his major investigations on his own. The method he devised is still of considerable value today: the fact-finding meeting.

"You can call a fact-finding meeting of people familiar with the situation in order to get at the source of what you call a difficult problem and come to know how it stands now, and then it will be easy to solve your difficult problem." A fact-finding meeting should have a specific agenda because *"you cannot*

possibly draw more or less correct conclusions at such meetings if you put questions casually instead of raising key-questions for discussion." Careful consideration should be given to its composition and size, especially the inclusion of older people "*because they are rich in experience and not only know what is going on but understand the causes and effects.*"

Fact-finding meetings are an effective and efficient means for visitors or newcomers to China to become familiar with the complex business environment. Many companies organize them for visiting executives, inviting a group of China-based managers from the same industry to a roundtable discussion of the problems and issues they face in their China operations. Sometimes these are relatively objective events and sometimes they have an underlying agenda, like Mao's "Hunan Report," and are intended to deliver a message that headquarters is not accepting from internal sources. Mao's advice on having a specific outline is rarely followed—but ought to be. His suggestion to carefully consider the composition of such a meeting is also relevant; it is important, for instance, that such gatherings should not consist only of expatriates or overseas Chinese as sometimes happens.

EXCHANGE INFORMATION

Executives who are based in China must also work hard to stay abreast of rapidly changing market conditions and ever-shifting regulatory practices. The best way to do this is to "'*Exchange information.'* *This means that members of a Party committee should keep each other informed and exchange views on matters that have come to their attention. This is of great importance in achieving a common language. Some fail to do so and, like the people described by Lao Tzu, 'do not visit each other all their lives, though the crowing of their cocks and the barking of their dogs are within hearing of each other.' The result is that they lack a common language.*"

Unfortunately, employees of modern multinationals often behave much like Lao Tzu's villagers of two thousand years ago—though the ringing of their cell phones and the droning of their computers are within hearing of each other, they fail to visit each other. Corporations and executives who wish to prosper in China must regularly and systematically exchange information with colleagues in their own company, in their industry, and with customers, suppliers, officials and anyone else who might provide some insight to changing market, political or economic conditions.

Mao's faith in the power of investigation was so strong that he believed any problem could be solved if the investigation into it was thorough enough. "*Investigation may be likened to the long months of pregnancy, and solving a problem to the day of birth. To investigate a problem is, indeed, to solve it.*" And, indeed, a myriad of perplexing problems can be solved through investigation.

One manufacturing company investigated why its managers were so loath to conduct performance reviews—and discovered that virtually everyone in the factory was related. Another company ran into problems when the frozen products it shipped in refrigerated train cars suddenly began to arrive melted. Upon investigating, it discovered that the railway bureau had begun a bonus program for conserving diesel; savvy train operators turned off the refrigeration units to earn the bonus. Once the company began to pay for diesel itself, its product again arrived frozen. Even deeper investigation was required for a commercial cake frosting company when its sales took a precipitous plunge. The problem, it discovered after considerable probing, was a superstitious rumor connecting birthday celebrations to death. In this particular case, investigation did not solve the problem— the company had to wait for an anti-feudal superstition campaign to dispel the fear and revitalize cake sales.

The process of mastering what you do not know in China is an unending one, as even Mao himself knew. But when you are having problems—or even when you're not—make sure to

> *Just get moving on your two legs, go the rounds of every section placed under your charge and "inquire into everything" as Confucius did, and then you will be able to solve the problems, however*

*little is your ability; for although your head may be
empty before you go out of doors, it will be empty no
longer when you return but will contain all sorts of
material necessary for the solution of the problems,
and that is how problems are solved.*

GUARD AGAINST ARROGANCE

One of the biggest stumbling blocks to mastering
what you do not know and succeeding in China is
arrogance. Arrogance interferes with your ability to
learn and puts off those from whose knowledge and
experience you could benefit. Mao knew this intel-
lectually and warned against it repeatedly.

*Guard against arrogance. For anyone in a lead-
ing position, this is a matter of principle...Even
those who have made no serious mistakes and
have achieved very great success in their work
should not be arrogant.*

But, while he remained ever vigilant for signs of
arrogance in his colleagues, Mao ultimately succumbed to it himself, with tragic results. In this, as
in so many other things, Mao in his later years
became what he often called others: "*a good teacher
by negative example.*"

Successful executives and corporations must
struggle against the assumption that they have China
figured out. Arrogant corporations (and individuals)

tend not to share information with others, to drop out of associations, and even refuse to work with their own governments. Going it alone when you are at the top of your game may work, but the day will come when every company needs help. Those with a reputation for arrogance are going to get less support from their industry and their government and may even find that they have irritated key officials in the Chinese government as much as everyone else.

A CRYSTALLIZATION OF COLLECTIVE WISDOM

Now let's consider how Mao's advice on mastering new subjects and carrying out investigations can be applied to your work in China today.

- **TALK TO A VARIETY OF PEOPLE.**
  If you are undertaking an investigation of any sort—or simply trying to stay atop your industry—talk to people outside your regular circle of colleagues, consultants, and buddies. In carrying out his Xunwu investigation, Mao talked to many people and spent

several weeks grilling a local party secretary, a poor peasant, a middle peasant, a former tax collector and a general store owner. *"A man should work in many fields, have contact with all sorts of people. Leftists should not only meet leftists but also rightists. They should not be afraid of this and that. I myself have met all sorts of people; I have met big officials and small ones."* To succeed in China, you must do the same.

• **MAKE STUDY A COMPONENT OF YOUR WORK.**

Most China-based executives are so busy that they consider themselves lucky to answer their email. The idea of taking on extra study—like learning Chinese, studying Chinese history, or becoming personally involved in investigative work—may seem impossible. But study is an essential element of success in China—and virtually everyone around you is engaged in it. Even China's top Communist Party leaders take a month out of their schedules each year to attend the Communist Party School. While some of their study is devoted to politics and ideology, much more of it is reportedly spent studying business, international relations, global economics, and, if need be, even how to use computers and send email. Continuing study is an old tradition—emperors had to engage in public study sessions with their tutors—that has been adapted by the Communist

Party and is worthy of emulation. As Mao said, "*Comrades, I study with determination, and I will go on studying until I die; when I die, that will be the end of it! In sum, as long as I am alive I shall study every day. Let us all create an environment of study.*"

- **GO DOWN TO THE COUNTRYSIDE.**

  Mao believed that one of the shortcomings in his investigations had been "*the undue stress on the countryside to the neglect of the towns*" because he and his comrades had "*descended physically*" but were "*still up in the mountains mentally.*" For many China executives, the problem is the opposite—their focus is all on the major cities and they know little about tertiary cities, and nothing about the countryside. This is a mistake—rural residents are moving into cities across China, the countryside and city are bleeding together, and transportation improvements are making previously remote areas accessible. It is essential to consider the distinct needs of rural and semi-rural residents—including those who have moved to cities—if you are going to expand your market.

- **GET OFF YOUR HORSE.**

  "*If one rides a horse to view the flowers...one cannot understand a problem profoundly even after a lifetime of effort.*" Likewise, if you stay in your chauffeur-driven car and your villa in a gated compound, you will never, after a lifetime of effort, come close to understanding China. One longtime expatriate manager practiced something he called "MBWA"—management by walking around. He walked the streets of Shanghai for several hours before dawn each morning and he walked around his company every day talking to people and observing. He did not speak Chinese, but he had a deep understanding of the way things worked and his company was profitable year in and year out.

- **DIG DEEPER.**

Don't stop investigating when you hear what you want to hear or get an answer that seems reasonable. Instead, ask different versions of the same questions and then ask questions that may seem irrelevant, counterintuitive, or downright silly. Don't just ask, for example, the price of the electricity that will power your factory—ask what power plant it comes from, ask if the plant exists, and then ask to see it. More than one company has been surprised to find out that the power price given them was accurate, but that the plant did not yet exist—and they were expected to help pay to build it. Similar scenarios abound—you will never regret spending extra time to ask extra questions.

- **Understand how your China business is perceived in headquarters.**

  If you are involved in the China side of a China business, you must understand how your operations are perceived back home, since this links directly to the support you'll receive. Some businesses struggle against the home office perception that they are an expense, rather than profit, center; others have line workers back home who fault made-in-China goods for political reasons. Some must compete with their corporation's home country products that are exported to China, and some must struggle against home office strategies that undermine their own. (Headquarters may speak aggressively about IPR piracy, for example, while the China business may prefer to remain off-record and work behind the scenes or through intermediary organizations.) Even employee retention is affected by the home office perception of the China business—if it is obvious that headquarters doesn't really care about China, it can be hard to keep your best people.

- **Pay attention to off-balance sheet items.**

  Market analysis is critical if you are looking to acquire a Chinese company, but so are issues like the company's management practices, personnel issues, government relationships, and the regulatory environment. Many companies neglect to investigate these, and they regret it down the road.

- **INVESTIGATE YOUR INVESTIGATORS.**
Since much investigation work is outsourced, it is crucial to understand the experience, skills, expertise, biases, work load, potential conflicts of interest, and so forth of those you hire. Check references, talk to other clients—investigate your investigators with the same diligence that you hope them to use on your behalf. Outsourced investigation work of any sort should also be analyzed and interpreted. Chances are, the company to whom you are outsourcing is also outsourcing to multiple other companies, and much can get lost in the process.

- **BE REALISTIC WITH YOUR ESTIMATES.**
Companies that are new to China often overestimate the true market size for their product or service and underestimate the competition; the costs of starting and running a business; and the time it will take to do just about everything, from negotiating a deal to becoming profitable. Estimates that are wildly off can significantly impact your prospects in China, or even derail them—headquarters have little patience with businesses that spend money lavishly on five-star hotels and business-class tickets but then fail to develop the promised market for their product within the proposed timeframe. If,

on the other hand, your estimate of potential market size or profits is too low, it may be difficult to get headquarters to give you the support you need.

• **TEST THE WATERS.**

The Chinese government uses pilot projects to test new ideas before implementing them on a national scale. It has done this for virtually every major reform, from the creation of "special economic zones" that were open to foreign trade and investment back in 1979 to a current pilot project that gives farmers financial rewards for having fewer children and will be implemented on a national scale beginning in 2007. Starting small and testing the waters may not gain you as much attention from headquarters, but it is the safest way to ensure the ultimate success of your China venture.

• **DON'T RUSH.**

Mastering what you do not know takes time, but corporations and executives are often in a rush when it comes to China. This is understandable, since China itself is in such a rush, but the odds of success will increase if you take more time to understand and investigate your potential partner, acquisition, employee, market, and so forth. This doesn't mean watching from the sidelines as others invest, but it may mean traveling to China more often, spending more days there, conducting more market surveys, talking to more people, and initially conducting business in only one location—and then moving quickly when you feel like you have your feet on the ground. "The saying "Haste does not bring success" does not mean that we should not make haste, but that we should not be impetuous; impetuosity leads only to failure.

- **FIND A PASSION OUTSIDE YOUR WORK.**
The happiest—and wisest—China-based executives are arguably those who have China-related passions outside their work. They collect antiques, contemporary art, teapots, or Cultural Revolution-era kitsch; travel around China photographing vernacular housing or climbing mountains; become experts in some area of Chinese culture, like furniture, feng shui, or cricket fighting. Passions such as these may not relate directly to business, but they are one of the best ways to get out of the high rises and villas and into the "real" China and will invariably benefit the ease with which you function in China and the pleasure that you take in it and thus indirectly benefit your work.

NOTES:

We shall have to master what we do—Short, p. 440.

I had no special standard for judging schools—Snow, p. 143.

...I did not want to go to Europe—Snow, p. 151.

My office was so low that people avoided—Snow, p. 151.

Originally I was a feudalist and an advocate—"Talk on Questions of Philosophy," August 18, 1964.

Mao was an ardent student of philosophy—Snow, p. 94.

made up of the universal truth of Marxism—Schram, p. 82.

You can't solve a problem—"Oppose Book Worship," May 1930.

use the X-ray method and *I would very much like to study*—"Letter to Li Jinxi," June 7, 1920, in *Road to Power*, Volume I, p. 518.

without using a single copper—Snow, p. 146.

Most likely, my future livelihood—"Report on the Affairs of the New People's Study Society," 1921, in *Road to Power*, Volume II, p. 59.

I am not too concerned when I lose things—preface to "Report from Xunwu" (Trans. by Roger R. Thompson, Stanford University Press, 1990), p. 45.

The Cultural Book Society was initiated—"The Founding of the Cultural Book Society," July 31, 1920, in *Road to Power*, Volume I, p. 535.

I still did not completely understand—preface to "Report from Xunwu," p. 45–6.

Eight of ten barbers do not—"Report from Xunwu," p. 104.

hard-bitten lot of prostitutes—"Report from Xunwu," p. 112.

diploma mills and the young masters break away—"Report from Xunwu," p. 113–4.

Unless you have investigated a problem—"Oppose Book Worship," May 1930.

many people who the moment they alight—"Oppose Book Worship," May 1930.

For such views or criticisms—"Reform Our Study," May 1941.

Probe deeply. Anyone new to investigation—"Oppose Book Worship," May 1930.

Everyone with responsibility for giving leadership—"Oppose Book Worship," May 1930.

You can call a fact-finding meeting—"Oppose Book Worship," May 1930.

'Exchange information.' This means that members—"Methods of Work of Party Committees," March 13, 1949.

Investigation may be likened to the—"Oppose Book Worship," May 1930.

Just get moving on your two legs—"Oppose Book Worship," May 1930.

Guard against arrogance—"Methods of Work of Party Committees," March 13, 1949.

a good teacher by negative example—"Some Experiences in Our Party's History," September 25, 1956.

A man should work in many fields—Schram, p. 239.

The saying "Haste does not bring success—"The United Front in Cultural Work," October 30, 1944.

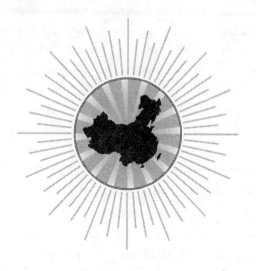

CHAPTER FIVE

ENEMIES AND FRIENDS

Who are our enemies? Who are our friends? This is a question of the first importance...

There are real friends and false friends. False friends are friendly on the surface, but say one thing and mean another. They dupe you...we shall be on guard against this.

Building strong, trusting, and respectful relationships is a crucial aspect of doing business in China, just as it is everywhere else in the world. Mao is hardly a model in this regard—although he certainly knew how to inspire great loyalty—but his approach to relationships nonetheless remains relevant because it continues to influence the conduct of government and business to this day.

A Man without Friends

Mao, by his own account, was from childhood an emotional and lonely person who "*never had good teachers or friends.*" As a student, he actually took out a newspaper advertisement to find friends; as an old man, he told Henry Kissinger he thought God didn't like him.

"*I am so driven by emotions that it is hard for me to live a disciplined life,*" he confessed in his mid-twenties, adding later, "*I constantly have the wrong attitude and always argue, so that people detest me.*"

Mao does indeed seem to have fallen out with nearly every friend he ever had. One of his earliest companions was Xiao Yu, the classmate with whom he spent a summer roaming Hunan, sleeping under trees and begging for rice at local farmhouses. But, the two later split and Mao (incorrectly) told Edgar Snow that Xiao Yu had "sold some of the most valuable treasures in the [Palace] museum and absconded with the funds in 1934." Xiao wrote a book about his time with Mao called *Mao Zedong and I Were Beggars* in which he describes a young Mao who was highly thoughtful and intelligent, but indeed very hard to get along with. In one episode, he describes Mao flying into a sarcastic rage and throwing a chair at a close friend whose loyalty he questioned during an argument over the historic novel *Three Kingdoms*.

This pattern continued throughout his life. In 1959, when his old comrade-at-arms and fellow Hunanese General Peng Dehuai wrote a balanced letter suggesting that the losses created by the Great Leap Forward were greater than the gains, Mao went ballistic. He distributed the private missive to members of the Party politburo and attacked Peng's views in front of everyone. The loyal general was subsequently purged for having had the temerity to speak the truth. He was arrested at the start of the Cultural Revolution, and he died in prison.

Being a member of Mao's family was to all appearances a worse fate than being his friend. Mao had two brothers and a sister; his sister was executed because of her relationship to him and his brothers both died fighting for the Communist cause. His first (excluding an arranged marriage which he rejected) wife Yang Kaihui was a Communist herself, but apparently wasn't happy at being left alone so often for the sake of revolution. When he was heading off for Canton in 1923, Mao wrote her a beautiful poem—but one that no wife would want to receive—in which he told her that he "*would like to be a rootless wanderer, and have nothing more to do with lovers' whispers."*

But by the late 1920s he had already wandered into the arms of the woman who would be his next wife. Yang Kaihui evidently knew her husband had found another when she was arrested by a Nationalist Party loyalist in 1930—but she still chose to be executed rather than renounce him. After her death their three sons were sent to Shanghai and left to fend for themselves—the youngest died and the other two lived on the streets for seven years. When the Communist Party finally found them, it sent them to Moscow and Mao did not see them for almost twenty years. One, Mao Anying, subsequently died during an American bombing raid while fighting in the Korean War and the other, who died in 2007, suffered from mental illness.

Mao's second wife, or "revolutionary companion," was a beautiful and spirited young woman named He Zizhen who joined the Communist Party at the age of sixteen while studying in a missionary school run by a Finnish nun. One of the few women to take part in the Long March, she marched pregnant, gave birth en route, and got shrapnel in her brain when she threw herself over a convalescent soldier to protect him during a bombing raid. She and Mao had six children together; one died in infancy, one lived to adulthood, and the exigencies of revolution forced them to abandon three because of the danger their crying might cause the troops.

When the Communist Party finally settled into a permanent base at the end of the Long March, Mao's flirting with pretty new revolutionary arrivals led to many quarrels. Upon learning that she was pregnant with their sixth child, the twenty-seven-year-old He decided she'd had enough. Ignoring Mao's pleas, gifts, and a direct Party order, she left for Moscow. There she gave birth to another son—who died before his first birthday, plunging her into despair. Mao arranged for her to return to China in 1947 and supported her for the rest of his life. But she was a broken woman, destined to battle mental illness and search in vain for her lost children; she and Mao apparently met again just once.

Mao's two children by his third wife, Jiang Qing, fared better than the others, although he was not close to either of these children. Likewise, Mao remained married to Jiang Qing until his death, but he apparently cheated on her with a harem of young women. She became a political power in her own right, the "white-boned demon" who led the Gang of Four and is blamed for much of the vindictive cruelty of the Cultural Revolution. She was arrested after Mao's death and put on trial where she famously proclaimed, "I was Chairman Mao's dog. What he said to bite, I bit." Her death sentence was never carried out, but she committed suicide in jail.

"Mao had no friends and was isolated from normal human contact," wrote his physician, Li Zhisui. "He spent little time with his wife and even less with his children. So far as I could tell, despite his initial friendliness at first meetings, Mao was devoid of human feeling, incapable of love, friendship, or warmth."

These are harsh words—and perhaps, by the end of his life, true. When it comes to relationships, the best you can say about Mao seems to be once again that he was "*a good teacher by negative example.*" But, Mao's attitude toward relationships is still important, because it influenced the creation and conduct of government in post-1949 China, and it does so to this day.

Mao's early years were spent in a Confucian society and he came of age in a Communist Party. As different as the two philosophies are, both emphasize relationships and give them primacy over laws and institutions—and it was in this sort of system that Mao functioned best. So when the PRC was established and the Communist Party set about creating institutions of government and a bureaucracy to run them, Mao resisted, preferring instead to govern (and manipulate) by way of his own relationship channels. Although some of his colleagues fought back and tried to strengthen the institutions of government, Mao ultimately won out; this is how his last wife, Jiang Qing, became one of the most powerful people in the nation and how all the institutions of government other than the military largely ceased to function for several years.

In the three decades since Mao's death, the Communist Party has made tremendous progress in strengthening the legal system and institutions of government. China is slowly moving from a nation ruled by men to a nation ruled by laws—albeit laws that are still often used as tools to protect the interests of the government rather than the people. As the process of institutionalization and legal reform accelerates, the importance of relationships gradually will diminish. In the meantime, however, most people still find relationships to be the most trustworthy and efficacious means for doing business. They take great care in forming, developing, and maintaining relationships—and if you want to succeed in China, you must do the same.

THE "G" WORD

Relationships in China are often referred to with the Chinese word *guanxi*. The Chinese term is used because it is more all-encompassing—including the ideas of trust, connections, and obligation—and more mysterious than plain old "relationships." Indeed, *guanxi* is sometimes discussed as though it were the magical key to success in China business— usually by people claiming to possess it and offering to use it on your behalf, for the right price. But don't let the "G" word fool you. *Guanxi* is important, but there is nothing mysterious about it. You can learn to navigate and build good relationships in China just as you do back home—and it doesn't have to cost you an arm and a leg.

Learning to Trust

When setting out to build relationships of any sort, think first of the questions that start this chapter: *"Who are our enemies? Who are our friends?"* This is the opening sentence of the first essay in the first volume of Mao's *Selected Works*, and many of the people you work with will know it. Figuring out who is an enemy and who is a friend is another way of asking who you can trust; this was one of Mao's greatest issues in life, and it is going to be one of yours if you work in China. Indeed, you will likely spend far more time than you can imagine trying to determine the trustworthiness of others and convince them of your own. Trust can be helped along by introductions—from friends, business contacts, or hired consultants—but ultimately it must be built by sharing meals, exchanging information and family photos, doing favors, engaging in formal negotiations, and just plain spending time together.

MISSED MESSAGES

Westerners are accustomed to direct communication and we often have difficulty detecting subtle messages.

But in China, indirect communication is the norm, especially when dealing with a sensitive topic.

The United States government learned this back when it was searching for a way to re-establish contact with China (to counter the Soviet threat) after many years of cold silence. Mao, of course, had the same idea in mind, so in 1970, he invited Edgar Snow to join him in viewing National Day celebrations in a highly visible spot atop the rostrum of the Gate of Heavenly Peace. Mao assumed the U.S. would realize the presence of an American at such an event was a clear signal that he wanted to talk. But the U.S. government missed the message completely. The start of a new relationship had to wait until the following year when Beijing invited the entire U.S. ping-pong team to Beijing immediately following a tournament in Japan. This invitation—coupled with Zhou Enlai's warm toast to the young athletes in the Great Hall of the People—was understood. Within months, Henry Kissinger was secretly visiting Beijing to lay the groundwork for a summit between Mao and Nixon.

Yet despite his recent experience with a missed message from Mao, Kissinger again failed to notice that Mao was trying to tell him something with his insistent references to exporting China's surplus women to the United States.

As Kissinger later explained, "But Mao was not yet sure that I had got the point; he returned to the

theme a few minutes later...Since Americans were
notoriously slow-witted, Mao returned to the
theme yet again—by which time I understood he
was making a point, though not yet what. After-
ward, Winston Lord's wife, Bette [who is Chinese-
American], explained it to me: that conditions in
China were far from being as stable as they looked;
that women—meaning Mao's wife, Jiang Qing, as
leader of the radical faction—were stirring up
China and challenging the prevailing policy."

If a consummate diplomat like Kissinger can
miss subtle messages, so can the rest of us. So when
trying to understand what your counterpart really
wants, always listen and look for hidden meanings.

If mutual trust is essential to establishing a relationship, mutual benefit is the key to sustaining it; as much
as Mao talked about trust, he talked about *"mutual benefit"* even more. (His successors have put both ideas
together in the catch phrase, "mutual trust and mutual
benefit" and made it a linchpin of China's diplomatic
relationships.) To achieve mutual benefit, you must
understand not only what your counterparts can do for
you, but what they want from you. Are they looking for
you to make them rich? Salvage a failing enterprise?
Boost their career or promotion prospects? Transfer
advanced technology? Help develop an industry? Get
their kid into an English program in Australia or a

boarding school in Britain? Once you think you know what they really want, you must decide how far you can go in providing it; the more you can help them realize their goals, the better the odds that your relationship will succeed.

SOME MAOIST NEGOTIATING TIPS

1. *Melons ripen. Don't pick them when they are not yet ripe. When they are ready, they will just drop off.*

To form a relationship based on *"mutual trust"* and *"mutual benefit"* takes considerable time and patience; attempting to rush the process will generally do you no good.

2. *The enemy wants to fight a short war, but we just will not do it. The enemy has internal conflicts. He just wants to defeat us and then to return to his own internal battles...*

Resist pressure to hurry negotiations—agree to a deal only when you are ready and the circumstances seem most advantageous to you.

3. If your counterpart is stalling and you want to make a deal, apply tactical pressure yourself.

Mao did this when he went to Moscow just weeks after liberation to negotiate a new Sino-Soviet Friendship Treaty with Stalin. A new treaty was very important to Mao but Stalin was in no hurry to replace the old one, which had been negotiated with the Nationalist Party and was beneficial to the USSR. So Stalin kept Mao waiting—for two months. Indeed, Mao's visit was so long that the international press began to speculate he was being held hostage. *"Finally, I got mad and said, 'If you don't want to negotiate, then let's not negotiate. I'll go home.'"* It would have been just as embarrassing for Mao to return to Beijing without a new treaty as for Stalin to let him go, but Mao called Stalin's bluff and got the treaty he wanted. (Albeit with some hidden strings attached.)

4. Put your negotiating partner out of his element.

When Khrushchev visited Beijing in 1958, Mao insisted on meeting in his swimming pool—even though he knew the Soviet leader couldn't swim. Completely unmoored, Khrushchev used a swim ring to stay afloat while Mao literally swam circles around him. Mao also chain smoked while meeting Khrushchev even though he knew the Soviet leader detested cigarette smoke. So if you ever find yourself with a negotiating counterpart at a banquet table swimming in liquor and swirling with cigarette smoke, think of Khrushchev—and don't agree to anything.

5. Good negotiating requires good acting.

Mao was well known for his situational ability to display anger, joy, frustration and sorrow and had a great talent for political theater. Think of your negotiating counterparts as a cast; everyone has a role to play and it is likely that they will remember all their lines—and yours. As Henry Kissinger aptly observed, "Every visit to China was like a carefully rehearsed play in which nothing was accidental and yet everything appeared spontaneous. The Chinese remembered every conversation, from those with the lowliest officials to those with the most senior statesman. Each remark by a Chinese was part of a jigsaw puzzle, even if at first our more literal intelligence did not pick up the design."

6. If you aren't good at negotiating, delegate the task to someone who is.

Mao had no patience for detailed negotiations in his old age and did not pretend otherwise. He repeatedly brushed off Nixon's attempts to discuss detailed diplomatic issues, telling him bluntly, "*Those questions are not questions to be discussed in my place. They should be discussed with the premier. I discuss philosophical questions.*"

7. *Since we have agreed to hold negotiations, we should be prepared for the many troubles which will arise after the success of the negotiations, and we should be ready with clear heads to deal with the tactics the other side will adopt, the tactics of the Monkey who gets into the stomach of the Princess of the Iron Fan to play the devil.*

The Monkey to whom Mao refers is the famous Monkey King in the novel *Journey to the West*. In one memorable scene, the Monkey turned himself into an insect and leapt into the stomach of the Princess of the Iron Fan, sickening and thereby defeating her. Mao presumably used this example because he knew from experience that in negotiating in China, no holds are barred—if your counterpart could turn into an insect and jump into your belly, he would—and the signing of an agreement means the beginning of the real problems, not the end.

8. *As long as we are fully prepared, we can beat any devilish Monkey.*

Preparation is essential to successful negotiations. When Mao met with Kissinger and Nixon in the early 1970s, he was in failing health—and in fact had nearly died. But, he was nonetheless extraordinarily well prepared for his meeting, displaying an easy familiarity not just with the international situation, but with the intricacies of U.S. domestic politics. "It was astonishing how much the aged leader knew about the domestic politics of faraway countries and how he could move inexorably to his conclusions without a note in front of him," wrote Kissinger. The better prepared you are, the more likely you are to succeed in your goals.

9. Arguments are an important part of the negotiation process.

Chairman Mao: *Did you finish your quarrel yet? Quarrels are good for you.*

Prime Minister Tanaka: We have had amiable talks.

Chairman Mao: *Truly good friends are made only by quarrels.*

10. *We should not refuse to enter into negotiations because we are afraid of trouble and want to avoid complications, nor should we enter into negotiations with our minds in a haze. We should be firm in principle; we should also have all the flexibility permissible and necessary for carrying out our principles.*

Make sure your home office has a copy of this quote when you prepare to negotiate in China.

Political Work

After you've established trust and mutual benefit (or at least their possibility) you can go on to build—and maintain—a relationship. The nature and number of these will depend on a variety of factors, including the size and scope of your business and how long your corporation has been in China. But, no matter what you are doing in China or how long you have been there, one of your most important relationships will be with the government itself. Mao wanted it that way—and so do his successors. "*Red and expert, politics and business are the unification of two pairs of opposites…There is no doubt that politics and economy, and politics and technology should be united…To pay no attention to politics and to be fully occupied with business matters is to become*

a perplexed economist or technician. And that is dangerous."
Although you no longer have to be "red" to succeed in China, you do court danger if you remain perplexed about politics. A government entity may well be your regulator, your customer, your sponsor, your competitor, your partner—or some combination of these. You must make the government your friend.

Building a friendly and productive relationship involves developing a deep understanding of the structure of the government, the Communist Party, and the complex symbiotic relationship that binds the two together. This is a challenging and time-consuming process. Since politics is serious business in China— *"war without bloodshed"*—many companies approach it with something resembling a battle plan, poring over organization charts for the government as a whole and for every ministry relevant to its business, creating influence maps to understand which government entities and individuals might affect its operations, and then setting up a system for interacting with those that are relevant.

TOO MANY HATS?

Responsibility in the Chinese government is opaque and overlapping. This dates to the revolutionary era when ranking Communist Party members were by necessity military officials, political leaders, economic planners, and cultural czars. Mao made battle plans, wrote political theory, drafted social policies, and set artistic guidelines. Soldiers grew food and farmers carried guns; musicians gave concerts one day and carried out land reform the next. After 1949, it was no longer necessary for individuals to wear so many hats, and there were attempts to clarify responsibility in the process of institutionalization.

The problem, of course, was that Mao hated bureaucracy, opposed institutionalization, and liked wearing many hats—and essentially desired a nation in his image. Under his rule, students went to labor in the countryside and laborers went to school. His doctor read policy papers, his bodyguards organized rectification meetings, his young assistants shared his bed, and his fellow leaders were left so desperate to know what he was thinking that they actually bugged his private train car. (The bugging was revealed when a technician teased a young woman who had just shared Mao's bed; the mortified woman promptly told Mao, who was furious.)

Despite the massive reforms China has undergone in the past three decades, officials can still intervene in areas well beyond their purview and obstruct almost at will. This means that a government relations plan must go beyond org charts and take into account the professional backgrounds, personal interests, and ephemeral whims of ranking officials in your geographic area or industrial sector.

Some companies work with outside consultants who specialize in government relations, others set up in-house government relations departments, and some do both. But, whichever route you take, building and maintaining relationships with the cornucopia of ministries, bureaus, administrations, commissions, and other government agencies that can affect your business will require your considerable personal involvement. It should also include regular communication with the government affairs function in your home market; efforts that your headquarters undertakes to furthering your nation's business relationship with China can be used to build trust and earn favors in Beijing.

The basis for a constructive government relationship is the same as with any other: mutual trust and benefit. Getting the various government agencies to trust you involves considerable education—you must learn what they need and show them how you can provide it. This means aligning yourself with the government's goals and plans and demonstrating how your corporation is best suited to help achieve these. It also means building individual relationships with relevant government officials, understanding the pressures they are under (and trying to help alleviate them), and maybe even assisting them with their own professional goals. This can take many legal and morally proper forms, including information sharing, seminars, assistance drafting regulations, and overseas study tours. Perhaps an official needs help in understanding an overseas market where your company has a strong position—or maybe he just needs advice on whether his daughter should go to Stanford or Harvard. Once you have a strong relationship, you can lobby on specific issues of importance to your business, handle any problems that arise, and keep atop changing regulations that will affect your industry.

TAKING IT TO THE TOP

Multinational executives often seek to meet top-level Chinese leaders in the hope that this will further their business interests. To attain these hard-to-get meetings, they sometimes employ the costly services of former ambassadors, secretaries of state, prime ministers, and presidents. It is fairly certain this is not a tactic Mao would have used or endorsed.

On the contrary, although he was the head of the Communist Party and the ruler of China—the most powerful individual in the entire nation—Mao still found it so hard to get anything done in Beijing that he regularly boarded his private train and traveled around the country doing government relations work with provincial officials. If Mao himself recognized that it is provincial and local officials who hold the real power, you should too.

Should you—or your CEO—remain hell bent on a meeting at the top, keep in mind that any access gained will prove fleeting unless you parlay it into a long-term relationship with your appropriate counterpart at the appropriate level. And take full advantage of those pricey consultants you hire—they could teach you far more of value about the machinations of the Chinese government than you'll ever learn from the thirty-minute photo op they help you arrange.

When it comes to working with the government on troublesome issues—like intellectual property protection—many companies wisely borrow Mao's united front strategy. By joining together in a large group (usually organized through a membership association based on nationality or industry) they can share resources, gain greater attention for their cause, and shield themselves from criticism for taking a public stance on a sensitive topic. Building a united front is not easy—Mao certainly did not enjoy working with his archenemy Chiang Kai-shek—but it is often the most pragmatic means to an end. In a similar vein, executives of multinational corporations should adopt a united front and avoid publicly questioning or contradicting their company's stated China policy. Such public contradictions happen more than you might expect—a recent example is the late 2006 comment by a Microsoft executive that his company would have to "decide if the persecuting of bloggers reaches a point that it's unacceptable to do business" in China. Microsoft quickly issued a statement calling the quotation "inaccurate" and reaffirming its intention to remain in China. A diversity of opinions is natural in a large organization, but when high-level executives comment publicly on the corporation's China business, they should speak with one voice.

Always remember, *"Political work is the life-blood of all economic work. This is particularly true at a time when the social and economic system is undergoing a fundamental change."*

Attend to the Newspapers

A second relationship of growing importance for foreign companies is that with the media. Mao—who, you'll remember, once wanted to be a reporter—recognized the significance of this early on. *"We must attend to the newspapers...it is necessary to call meetings of reporters, newspaper staffs and radio personnel to exchange views with them and inform them of the guiding principles in our propaganda."*

Nonetheless, it took Mao some time to bring the media completely to heel; the Beijing newspapers refused to publish the 1965 editorial that launched the Cultural Revolution for twenty days after it was carried in Shanghai. But when Mao finally got the press and its overlords to do a full kowtow, the papers became such staid and obedient propaganda organs that many foreigners think of them as such to this day.

In reality, however, the Chinese press, while hardly free, has advanced considerably in recent years, especially in covering business and economics. Newspapers have also become increasingly profit-oriented, and thus fond of scandal. Sex and politics are largely off-limits in the mainstream media, but consumerism and nationalism are politically and popularly acceptable substitutes. This means that any story that concerns a foreign company said to be cheating, deceiving, or otherwise badly treating Chinese consumers is certain to be hot, and spread like wildfire. To avoid becoming a scandal headline—especially if you are big, famous, or dominant—you must build a constructive relationship with targeted traditional media outlets and journalists.

Of equal or even greater importance is the Internet, specifically bulletin boards, chat rooms, and blogs. At the end of 2006, China officially had 137 million Internet users, with some estimates reaching toward 200 million. (The numbers are hard to count because many young people access the Internet by cell phone.) They are a passionate group who spend vast amounts of time online—one much-quoted estimate is 2 billion hours a week. More than 50 million people post or read messages on BBS sites, and as many as 80 million read or write blogs.

BEWARE THE WRATH OF THE BLOGOSPHERE

Most blogs in China are like those anywhere, full of family photos and quirky posts intended primarily for friends and family. But in a nation that lacks both freedom of speech and assembly, blogs currently provide a measure of both that is attractive to many—including those who wish to express deviant behavior or opinions and those who wish to denounce it. This dynamic has led to some well-publicized displays of vigilante justice and mob mentality—and has led some people to compare blogs to the "big-character posters" that were plastered across China by Red Guards during the Cultural Revolution.

In early 2006, for example, a woman posted video of herself dressed in a slinky cocktail dress and stiletto heels—which she used to crush a little black kitten to death. The millions of netizens who saw the images (which apparently are enjoyed by crushing fetishists) were infuriated. By way of concerted internet sleuthing, they managed to track down the woman in the northern province of Heilongjiang, harass her, and get her fired from her job—as a nurse. Another case of Internet vigilantism was directed at a British English teacher in Shanghai who blogged about his sexual exploits with Chinese women, mixed with whining comments about Chinese culture and Chinese men. A Shanghai academic saw the blog and became so incensed that he put out an internet call for "this piece of garbage" to be kicked out of China by National Day, 2006. (After a temporary silence, the "foreign scoundrel" continues to blog from China and the Shanghai professor has published a book that discusses his failed expulsion campaign, entitled *I'm Enraged*.)

Kitten crushers and sexual rakes may seem to deserve little sympathy, but the wrath of China's bloggers also includes multinationals. In fact, one of China's first blogs was created for the explicit purpose of attacking Microsoft. Its author, Fang Xingdong, had already penned a book called *Challenge Microsoft Hegemony* and became unhappy when his anti-Microsoft vitriol was removed from major websites. After starting his own blog to criticize Microsoft, he went on to found Bokee.com which is now one of China's largest blog sites. If Mao Zedong were alive today, he would almost certainly be a blogger.

Most Western interest in China's internet is focused on the censorship of subjects the government considers sensitive, like sex and politics. But for many foreign companies who operate in China, the Internet looks like a wild and freewheeling arena (which some no doubt only wish they could censor).

A growing number of multinationals have faced serious negative publicity that either originated or spread out of control on the Internet. In 2006, KFC and Volkswagen were both criticized online for offline advertisements intended to be humorous; as a result, KFC changed the ending of a television commercial and Volkswagen removed a subway advertisement. Carlyle Group's planned purchase of a large stake in a major Chinese machinery company was put on hold for months after a Chinese competitor used a blog to start a nationalistic campaign aimed at stopping the sale. In 2007, a popular CCTV anchorman used his personal blog to argue that Starbucks' six-year-old outlet in the Forbidden City was "inappropriate" because it contributed to the "erosion of Chinese culture." The blog posting received international attention and sparked a campaign to force Starbucks from the ancient imperial palace.

The computer manufacturer Dell was targeted when a customer discovered his laptop contained a processor that differed slightly from the one advertised, although it apparently did not affect the computer's performance. He posted his discovery on a BBS forum dedicated to laptops, found hundreds of others whose processors were also different than advertised and then initiated a class-action lawsuit against Dell. After the issue was covered by *People's Daily* and dubbed "processor gate," Dell offered refunds but discovered that the historic grievances motivating angry, online consumers are not so easily quieted. As *People's Daily* quoted one "legal expert" discussing the case, "If consumers win, it will force multinationals to soften their long-held arrogance toward Chinese consumers and make it easier for Chinese customers to protect their rights." (In the end, consumers didn't win on this one; the lawsuit was thrown out by a Chinese court in December of 2006.)

The Chinese government reportedly has more than thirty thousand people monitoring the Internet for content it fears could negatively impact its hold on power. Multinationals cannot—and obviously should not—become censors, but they can and should monitor, defend, and promote their corporate reputation on the Internet. Even better is to use the Internet as the democratic and equalizing tool it is intended to be by forging a stronger relationship with customers online. Some companies—including Pepsi, Nike, and Ponds—have begun to do this, inviting online consumers to help them create a marketing campaign, devise a promotion, or choose a new corporate spokesperson. Others use the Internet to monitor consumer comments, respond to feedback, conduct focus group surveys, and test consumer reaction to new marketing campaigns.

Building and maintaining strong relationships and relationship networks will greatly facilitate the ease with which you do business in China—and may prove invaluable in a crisis situation. Forging such relationships—with partners, suppliers, customers, regulators, employees, reporters, and more—entails a significant commitment of time and energy. Ultimately it requires you to always try to understand what motivates—or scares—your relationship counterparts by trying to see things from their perspective. *"In this world, things are complicated and are decided by many factors. We should look at problems from different aspects, not from just one."*

A CRYSTALLIZATION OF COLLECTIVE WISDOM

Now let's consider some specific tactics for building and maintaining productive working relationships.

- **UNDERSTAND DIFFERENT RISK-REWARD RATIOS.**
  The ratio of risk to reward will differ greatly among your various relationships. Most government officials, for example, are extremely risk averse since a single mistake can derail an entire career. Private entrepreneurs, on the other hand, are often willing to take tremendous risks to build a business. Understanding—and respecting—risk tolerance is a key aspect of building a strong working relationship.

- **REPLACE "WIN-LOSE" WITH "WIN-WIN."**

Mao's win-lose concept of trade and other business relationships still runs deep in China. Indeed, despite years of propaganda regarding the importance of "mutual benefit," many people still believe that every deal has a winner and a loser. You are likely to run up against this attitude in many negotiations, and it will be your responsibility to convince your counterpart that the deal can be a win-win one for both sides.

- **SILENCE IS GOLDEN.**

Chinese children are taught to sit at the dinner table and eat their food without talking; Westerners are taught to sit at the dinner table and make conversation over food. So when Westerners go to China they sit at a negotiating table and do as they have been trained since childhood—they talk. The Chinese come to the table comfortable with silence and prepared to talk only when they deem it necessary. Learning to be silent is almost as useful a negotiating tool as learning to listen.

- **PERIODICALLY REORIENT YOUR RELATIONSHIPS.**

The government, Party, and even state-owned enterprise officials with whom you build relationships will change more often than you'd like, whether because of promotion, transfer, retirement, or other reasons.

It is important to spread your relationship net wide to ensure that you are not left stranded when this happens. Take time with youthful officials who will rise up the ladder and keep atop the shifts brought about by political winds, government reorganizations, and the passage of time.

- **WATCH FOR SHIFTING ALLIANCES.**
The answer to the question, "Who are our enemies? Who are our friends?" is changing, rather than static. It can be affected by circumstances beyond your control, like domestic politics or foreign relations, or by your own business undertakings. If, for example, you try to acquire a Chinese company you may suddenly find that friends become enemies and companies that previously competed against each other are suddenly working together to stop your acquisition. Never assume that a friend will always be a friend or an enemy always an enemy.

- **BUILD RELATIONSHIPS FOR THE FUTURE.**
If you build relationships for your company, rather than just for yourself, you must strive to create bonds that will last decades by forming links with younger officials, executives, and even students who may go on to be key players in business and government. There is naturally a limit to how much of this

any one person can do. But at the very least, don't brush people off because they are young or lack power. Remember the grudge Mao bore against the *"busy men"* who had no time to speak to an assistant librarian speaking southern dialect?

- **NEGOTIATION IS AN OPPORTUNITY.**

Negotiation in China may be a tortuous process, but it is also a grand opportunity that won't last forever. The various levels of the Chinese government are still willing to negotiate many issues—tax breaks, special privileges—that would be largely non-negotiable in the West. If you are good at building relationships, you can use this willingness to negotiate to tremendous advantage.

- **SAVE FACE.**

Handle all relationships—even those that are contentious or that do not come to fruition—with courtesy, and never make someone lose face. If you embarrass or humiliate someone, even unintentionally, you will have turned a potential friend into an almost certain enemy.

- **BEWARE OF "OLD FRIENDS" YOU JUST MET.**

The phrase "old friend," or *"lao pengyou,"* is a loaded term that often precedes an effort to squeeze a concession out of you. Keep your resolve even when the toasts turn to your mutual friendship. As Henry Kissinger learned through his negotiations with Mao and colleagues, "Chinese use friendship as a halter in advance of negotiation; by admitting the interlocutor to at least the appearance of personal intimacy, a subtle restraint is placed on the claims he can put forward."

- **RELATIONSHIPS ARE THE KEY TO CRISIS MANAGEMENT.**
  In building your relationships, don't forget the people you might need in a crunch—the local Public Security Bureau, your own embassy or consulate, and any other agencies or organizations you can envision needing assistance from in case of emergency. More than one company has run into problems because they neglected to build relationships with these technically non-business contacts whose assistance could have proved business-saving in a crisis situation.

- **PUT MORE TIME INTO YOUR RELATIONSHIPS.**
  Relationships are not just about quality, they are also about quantity. The time spent building a relationship can seem wasted when you are eating yet another lavish banquet or traveling on yet another international flight for a one-hour meeting, but it is not. Indeed, almost every business—and every

relationship–will benefit from more time.

- **RELATIONSHIP BUILDING SHOULD NOT JUST BE LEFT TO THE CHINA OFFICE.**
High-level executives from back home should share the responsibility of building strong relationships in China. The payoff from such home office involvement is exponential, since it is respected by the Chinese and helps home office executives to better understand what is happening in China.

NOTES:

Who are our enemies—in "Analysis of the Classes in Chinese Society," March, 1926.

There are real friends and—in Short, p. 421.

never had good teachers—"Letter to his teacher Li Jinxi," 1915, in *Road to Power*, Volume I, p. 84.

I am so driven by emotions—"Letter to Li Jinxi," June 7, 1920, in *Road to Power*, Volume I, p. 518.

I constantly have the wrong attitude—in Spence, p. 61.

would like to be a rootless wanderer—in Spence, p. 66.

Mao had no friends and was isolated from—in Li Zhisui, p. 120.

But Mao was not yet sure—in Kissinger, *Years of Upheaval*, p. 68.

Melons ripen. Don't pick them—in Short, p. 379. (Similar quote in "The Debate on the Cooperative Transformation of Agriculture and the Current Class Struggle," October 11, 1955.)

The enemy wants to fight a short war—in Short, p. 255.

Finally, I got mad and said—in Li Zhisui, p. 117.

Those questions are not questions—in Kissinger Transcripts, p. 61.

Since we have agreed to hold negotiations—"Report to the Second Plenary Session of the Seventh Central Committee of the Communist Party of China," March 5, 1949.

As long as we are fully prepared—"Report to the Second Plenary Session of the Seventh Central Committee of the Communist Party of China," March 5, 1949.

It was astonishing how much—in Kissinger, Years of Upheaval, p. 691.

Did you finish your quarrel?—in Pye, *The Man in the Leader*, p. 127.

We should not refuse to enter into negotiations—"Report to the Second Plenary Session of the Seventh Central Committee of the Communist Party of China," March 5, 1949.

Red and expert, politics and business—"Red and Expert," January 31, 1958. (In *Long Live Mao Zedong Thought*, Red Guard Publication, 1969.)

war without bloodshed—in "On Protracted War," May 1938.

decide if the persecuting of bloggers reaches a point that it's unaccept-able to do business and "inaccurate"—Kristi Heim, "Microsoft out of China? Yeah, right." Tech Tracks, *Seattle Times*, November 2, 2006.

Political work is the life-blood—Introductory note to "A Serious Lesson," 1955 in *The Socialist Upsurge in China's Countryside*, Chinese ed., Vol. I.

We must attend to the newspapers—"Speech at the Second Plenary Session of the Eighth Central Committee of the Communist Party of China," November 15, 1956.

China officially has 137 million—lower figure according to China Internet Network Information Center, higher figure according to Charles Zhang, CEO of Sohu.com

If consumers win, it will force—People's Daily, August 24, 2006 (English, online).

In this world, things are complicated—"On the Chungking Negotiations," October 17, 1945.

Chinese use friendship as a halter—in Kissinger, *The White House Years*, p. 1056.

CHAPTER SIX

RESIST DOGMATISM

Those who regard Marxism-Leninism as religious dogma show...blind ignorance. We must tell them openly, 'Your dogma is of no use,' or, to speak crudely, 'Your dogma is of less use than dog——.' Dog——can fertilize fields and man's s——can feed dogs. But dogmas? They can't fertilize fields and they can't feed dogs. What use are they?

Many people come to China saddled with dogmatic notions about how best to do business in their industry. But no matter how dominant the company or experienced the executive, they can usually benefit by consciously adapting to the unique needs and practices of the China market, a process Mao called sinification.

Abolish Foreign Stereotypes

Mao viewed dogmatism as a threat to the Chinese revolution and fought it throughout his life.

His battle was perhaps at its most pitched in the early 1930s when he found himself at odds with a group of young Communists who had studied at Sun Yat-Sen University in Moscow and returned to China to dominate the Party's Central Committee. These "Returned Students" were well versed in Marxist theory and criticized Mao for being too easy on rich peasants, failing to develop a strong labor movement, and exhibiting "conservatism and flightism" by retreating from unwinnable battles and refusing to attack big cities.

Mao was at an apparent disadvantage when it came to defending himself against these charges and wrestling the Returned Students for control of the revolution. He hadn't gone to Moscow and didn't yet have his own significant body of Marxist theoretical interpretation with which to challenge theirs. But what he did have was years of practice organizing and fighting in China, an abiding belief that this mattered far more than book learning or foreign experience, and little patience for anyone who thought otherwise. So, when the Returned Student-dominated Central Committee gave him orders he didn't agree with, he declared that following mistaken directives was "*a form of sabotage*" and ignored them. In the spring of 1930 he was repeatedly asked to attend a conference in Shanghai but instead went off to Xunwu to conduct his investigation. And when the Central Committee ordered him to take the Red Army north in 1932, he marched south instead. His decision proved wise and the army took an important town in Fujian province, netting $500,000 cash, two Nationalist airplanes, and a stash of weaponry and ammunition in the process.

But though this was the first major military triumph in more than a year, the Returned Students on the Central Committee were livid that Mao had breached Party discipline and violated orders. Zhou Enlai, who had supported Mao's decision, criticized himself for this "very serious mistake" and promised it would not happen again. But Mao was not about to apologize. Instead, he fired off a telegram telling the Returned Students that "*The political appraisal and military strategy of the Center are wholly erroneous...To propose using last year's strategy under present circumstances is right opportunism.*" The Central Committee had charged Mao with these very same errors, and its members were not amused to have their own words used against them. Fed up, they removed Mao from his position as Commissar and barred him from all important military decisions for the next two years.

Without Mao, however, the fighting did not go well, and the Communist troops soon found themselves encircled by Nationalist Army units that blocked them in with long lines of stone forts. Mao twice suggested that the army break away and fight outside the block house on the mountainous terrain where it would have an advantage, but his "flightist" advice was ignored.

By 1934, the situation was so bad that it was decided to abandon the Soviet Republic the Communists had established. Mao was not involved in the decision, but he joined the eighty thousand marchers as they headed off on the tactical retreat that would become known as the Long March. Only a few thousand people would survive the now fabled six thousand mile, 370 day march, which took the Red Army through some of the world's most inhospitable territory and required its members to struggle against frostbite, malaria, unfriendly minority populations, exhaustion, and near starvation. But over the course of the march, Mao's military strategies were vindicated and his authority restored. He emerged from it in a position of political and military dominance which he would maintain for the rest of his life.

Looking back on this period, Mao proclaimed that the *"chief mistake"* of the Returned Students was dogmatism, or *"transplanting foreign experience mechanically,"* an error he would forever oppose. Instead, he would promote practice as *"the criterion of truth."* *"Whoever wants to know a thing has no way of doing so except by coming into contact with it, that is, by living (practicing) in its environment."* Mao's emphasis on practice is another example of his talent for turning weakness into strength, but he stuck with it even after he had risen to the top of the Party, continuing to insist that any ideology be rooted in China's reality. *"Foreign stereotypes must be abolished, there must be less singing of empty, abstract tunes, and dogmatism must be laid to rest, they must be replaced by the fresh, lively Chinese style and spirit which the common people of China love."* Over the course of the 1950s, he became increasingly unhappy about what he considered the Party's mindless transplantation of the Soviet Union's experiences. He even angrily told his doctor that his fellow leaders were *"a bunch of zombies with a slave mentality."* *"Marxism didn't just drop from heaven,"* he would complain. *"We shouldn't do everything according to the books, slavishly copying every word."*

Yet, though he battled it throughout his life, Mao never managed to defeat dogmatism—on the contrary, he succumbed to his own homegrown version of it. Even while accusing his colleagues of dogmatically copying the Soviet Union to build the bureaucratic, educational, and industrial framework of New China in the 1950s, Mao dogmatically insisted on using such old, ideologically-based methods as class struggle and mass movements. These had worked well to achieve Party goals in the revolutionary era, but they were ill-suited to building a stable socialist society. When Mao still clung to his old methods even after the disaster of the Great Leap Forward, Deng Xiaoping declared bluntly that "We have launched many large-scale movements in recent years...It is not good to have movements so frequently." But Mao refused to listen; practice increasingly became irrelevant if it didn't buttress his ideology. Instead, he prepared to launch the biggest mass movement of them all, the Cultural Revolution.

During the Cultural Revolution, Mao allowed his own theories to become the ultimate dogma, a near religious creed. More than 40 billion volumes of his works were printed during this time, or fifteen books for every person in China. Virtually everyone owned at least one copy of *Quotations from Chairman Mao*, better known in the West as "The Little Red Book," and many felt obligated to memorize it. (Many, my husband among them, can still recite it from memory with a prompt to start each quotation.) Every movie, meeting, theatrical performance, business letter, and airplane flight in China began with a Mao quotation. Mao's image was as sacred as his word—in the first three years of the Cultural Revolution, between 2.5 and 5 billion Mao badges were manufactured, and virtually everyone wore one pinned over his heart every day. Production of the badges ended in 1969 when Mao himself declared that it was a waste of metal that could be better used to build airplanes; even he knew that the veneration of his dogma and person had gotten out of control.

Mules Are Good

Unfortunately, China seems to bring out dogmatic tendencies even in generally non-dogmatic people—just as it did in Mao. The first Europeans to have a significant impact on Chinese society were missionaries bent on converting the Chinese to Christianity. They were followed by untold numbers of mercenaries, traders, diplomats, and ordinary Westerners who all assumed China would be better off if it looked and acted more like their nations—an attitude that persists to this day. Multinationals that invest in China are often equally dogmatic, certain that their business methods, products, processes, or services are superior. Executives, too, tend to assume that their knowledge of international business and developed markets gives them an edge over their Chinese peers. Such assumptions usually grow stronger for a time and then gradually fade as corporations face intense competition from Chinese companies and executives realize their approach is not having the desired impact. If they are wise, they then begin to question their dogmas and consider a new approach. As an Australian executive based in China told me, "I came to China not knowing a thing about it and it took me a while to realize that either China had to change or I had to change."

CHANGING CHINA

This dogmatic desire to change China remains especially strong in the U.S. where the belief that China should be more like America transcends political party. When President Clinton visited Shanghai in 1998, China-based diplomats were sent scrambling to find a peasant family that lived in a freestanding house with a mortgage in an environmentally correct village with a recycling plant or an organic farm and a democratically elected leader who won in an election that included more than one candidate. The idea, it seemed, was for voters back home to see that the U.S. "engagement policy" was succeeding in making China more like America. When no such village was found, the idea was dropped—seeing how Chinese villagers really lived was not a priority. As a presidential candidate, George Bush echoed similarly dogmatic sentiments when he explained, "Trade with China will promote freedom. The case for trade is not just monetary, but moral—not just a matter of commerce, but a matter of conviction. Economic freedom creates habits of liberty. And habits of liberty create expectations of democracy." Trade with China has not yet brought democracy and odds are it never will—but our dogmatic desire to change China in our own image will undoubtedly stay intact.

Once practice and experience have shown that the mechanical transplantation of foreign experience doesn't usually work, there is a ready solution: sinification, meaning adapting your practices to China's reality. Mao sinified Marxism by adapting it to China's circumstances, and foreign companies must do the same to their businesses. *"We must plant our backsides on the body of China...When we study China, we must take China as the center..."* Sinification does not mean rejecting everything you did back home or trying to become Chinese; some foreign things can be transplanted quite successfully to China, while others will succeed better with some adaptation. And some things should not be sinified no matter what—like your core company (or personal) values.

Sinification is a challenging process. Although Mao's sinification of Marxism is now considered one of his major contributions to China and to Communism, he had to battle the Returned Students for several years to get his views accepted. If it was hard for

Mao, it will likely be hard for you, too. Indeed, some China-based multinational executives oppose sinification on principle, just as the Returned Students did.

THE ARGUMENT AGAINST SINIFICATION

Opponents of sinification generally argue in favor of internationalization. The Returned Students emphasized that China's revolution was part of the international Communist movement, just as some multinational executives argue that global and Chinese corporations alike should be making themselves more international, not more local. Indeed, some executives are upset by the mere suggestion that their hard-earned and highly-compensated experience could benefit by being more Chinese.

"The Chinese keep saying that we need to do it the 'Chinese way,'" one American joint venture manager complained to *The Financial Times*. "There is no Chinese way in building or designing....Okay? Industry is a science. It has nothing to do with Mao Zedong, the Qing dynasty or Chinese history. This is science. You can argue about the history of the world all you want but one plus one has to equal two."

Had this frustrated executive studied his Mao, he would know that industry in the real world is inseparable from practice—and that in China this does still relate to Mao Zedong and history. Indeed, he might even learn to question his own assumption that one plus one always equals two; Mao once launched an ideological battle over the premise that *"one divides into two."*

More importantly, he would know—as should we all—that sinification and globalization are not mutually exclusive goals; instead, they are a unity of opposites. As Mao said, *"To separate internationalist content from national form is the practice of those who do not understand the first thing about internationalism."*

Even when China-based executives do recognize the need to adapt to China, headquarters can prove a stumbling block, opposing efforts to "go native" just as Moscow sometimes opposed Mao's sinified strategies. But to go to China and not even consider adapting your business or yourself to the local market is a major mistake—a degree of sinification will benefit any corporation or individual aiming to succeed.

BOMBARD THE HEADQUARTERS!

Mao rebelled against headquarters from his earliest years—as a child when he threatened to drown himself after his father beat him; as a student when he dropped out of school because he didn't like the rules; as a guerilla when he disobeyed orders from the Communist Party in Shanghai; and as head of the Communist Party when he called for Red Guards to *"Bombard the headquarters!"*—even though he himself was the headquarters.

Unfortunately, many China-based executives can relate to Mao's exasperation with headquarters even if they would not condone his methods for dealing with it. Indeed, the difficulty of working with head-quarters—whether because they are slow, bureaucratic, unrealistic, unsupportive, excessively demanding, or just plain China-ignorant—is one of the most frequently voiced complaints that China-based executives make. While some disconnects between the home office and China businesses are natural, the relationship is one that both sides would do well to better manage.

If you are based in China, it is your job to help sinify headquarters—or at least sensitize them to the way things work so your home-based bosses and colleagues can better understand the pressures you are under. And if you are the headquarters, it is your job to understand as best you can the realities and pressures of doing business in China so that you can give your China-based executives the prompt support they need—and avoid bombardments of any sort.

Successful sinification entails many of the general issues discussed already in this book—an understanding of China's modern history and sense of grievance; an acceptance of the unity of opposites; a willingness to align one's goals with those of the government; a deep understanding of local market conditions and consumer preferences gained through investigation; a capacity for building and maintaining a network of relationships with employees, customers, partners, and government overseers. It also requires the ability to question one's own established dogma, experiment with new ideas, and link oneself with the masses. As Mao put it, *"There are two principles here: one is the actual needs of the masses rather than what we fancy they need, and the other is the wishes of the masses, who must make up their own minds instead of our making up their minds for them."*

A surprising number of multinationals still make the mistake of thinking they can decide what the masses want. They adhere to home country product specifications and home country prices, both of which may prove too high for the market; or they assume that an inexpensive, lower quality product that sells well in another developing country—like a cheap car—will also do well in China, forgetting that Chinese consumers will stretch their budgets when it comes to high-visibility objects and reject those that appear obviously cheap. But, if some companies fail to consider the "actual needs of the masses," many others have successfully sinified their products along the lines of this advice that Mao gave Chinese musicians in 1956: *"You can produce some things which are neither Chinese nor Western. If what comes out is neither a donkey nor a horse but a mule, that would be not bad at all."*

Some examples of successful *"mules"* include Häagen-Daaz green tea ice cream; Starbucks coffee mooncakes; and Mr. Donut's red bean donuts. L'Oreal sells skin-whitening cream and is constructing a research and development center in Shanghai that will focus on integrating traditional Chinese medicine and herbs into cosmetics. IKEA stores in China have a section for balcony furniture and Carrefour sells live fish. One joint venture even produced a washing machine that is strong enough to clean sweet potatoes. Sinified marketing and sales techniques are also increasingly common. At its Chongqing store, Wal-Mart holds daily activities for retirees, runs shuttle buses to nearby housing developments, and offers live "retail-tainment" at which school groups perform. Its managers have also discovered that there is a positive correlation between noise and sales, so when they want to get the cash registers ringing, they reportedly send someone out to make as much noise as possible while restocking shelves or creating a new display.

Sinifying practices and processes is perhaps even harder than sinifying products, but equally crucial. Mao faced this problem when he was creating battle strategies to fight the Japanese and the Nationalists:

> *Some people...say that it is enough merely to study the experience of revolutionary war in Russia...and the military manuals published by Soviet military*

> *organizations. They do not see that these...manuals*
> *embody the specific characteristics of the...Soviet*
> *Union, and that if we copy and apply them mechan-*
> *ically without allowing any change, we shall...be* —
> *'cutting the feet to fit the shoes,' and will be defeated.*

Many multinationals are also guilty of cutting the feet to fit the shoes—they translate training manuals into Chinese without modification, for example, and then apply them mechanically. Some argue that this works perfectly well, but common sense—not to mention the problems that multinationals have in keeping their best employees—would seem to suggest otherwise.

A big offender when it comes to mechanical transplantation is the very industry that should be setting an example for others—business schools. China has roughly one hundred MBA programs, virtually all of which use case studies created by Harvard Business School that discuss businesses outside China. This educational dogmatism has been criticized, and efforts to create a body of sinified case studies have begun. But mechanical transplantation includes more than written materials; indeed, some companies transplant entire factories to China. Their intentions are good—they want to build a world class factory—but the assumption that a "world class" factory in China must look exactly like one back home is erroneous. It may, for instance, make sense to take advantage of China's lower labor costs (and create more jobs, thus earning political favor) by building a factory that uses semi-automatic processes to make "world class" products. Factory and equipment design and construction can also be productively adapted to local conditions. One industrial gas company built a plant in China at a third of the U.S. cost in part because it used a compressor with a flywheel and a vertical CO_2 tank rather than a horizontal one. It wasn't fancy, but it worked; little sinifications can save big money.

The biggest challenge when it comes to sinification is to sinify your thinking and overall corporate approach to problem-solving because *"China's problems are complicated and our brains must also be a little complicated."* An important aspect of this is the ability to be flexible and move fast—neither of which are hallmarks of large corporations. Many executives of entrepreneurial Chinese companies—Huawei, Haier and Wahaha among them—actively study Mao's theory of guerrilla warfare and adapt it to business. Their strategy is *"that of a war of maneuver, over an extended, shifting and indefinite front: a strategy depending for success on a high degree of mobility in difficult terrain, and featured by swift attack and withdrawal, swift concentration and dispersal."* A multinational competing with an entrepreneurial Chinese business using guerilla tactics is akin to the huge Nationalist army with its superior technology, excessive baggage and conventional forces trying to hold a fixed position against the poorly-equipped but light-footed Red Army guerrillas who constantly changed tactics—and ultimately won the war. Sometimes conventional tactics work, and sometimes it's better to use guerrilla tactics—Mao triumphed as a military leader because he was willing and able to use both, and anyone who hopes to succeed in China must be similarly flexible.

A sinified outlook is also essential to coping with China's political environment. Because no matter how strong your government relations are, at some point your business is going to be impacted by politics. *"How can [anything be resolved] when only numbers are discussed, without politics? The relationship between politics and numbers is like that between officers and soldiers: Politics is the commander."* It is common, for instance, for cities to change all traffic regulations to accommodate a national holiday or a political event. When Shanghai hosted the Shanghai Cooperation Organization summit in the summer of 2006, it closed the Bund and ordered Bund-based businesses to shut down for two days while it staged fireworks displays for visiting dignitaries. More serious political interference is also possible, as when Beijing suddenly decided to ban direct sales in 1998, forcing companies such as Avon and Mary Kay Cosmetics to reinvent themselves overnight. (The ban was lifted in 2005.) But, if your outlook is sinified—meaning you understand that politics still takes precedence—you will be prepared for such political interference and will somehow survive.

GOVERNMENT BY CAMPAIGN

When Mao transitioned from military to civilian leadership, he brought a favored military tactic with him: the campaign. Mao used campaigns to create a sense of urgency and unity to achieve specific goals, be this the killing of sparrows or crushing of alleged counter-revolutionaries. Campaigns were also a technique in his battle against bureaucrats who he accused of *"tottering along like a woman with bound feet and constantly complaining, 'You're going too fast.'"*

Mao's successors still govern by campaigns. Sometimes these are politically-motivated—like the 1999 campaign against the Falungong sect which used many techniques straight out of the Cultural Revolution—and sometimes they serve important social interests, like campaigns against SARS, AIDS, crime, and improper English. Campaigns to encourage civilized behavior are held periodically, the most recent President Hu's "Eight Honors and Eight Disgraces," which borrows its style and some of its content directly from Mao.

Government campaigns have different aims, but they are all alike in their use of massive resources and extensive propaganda. When Shanghai launches its periodic campaigns against jay-walking, for instance, it tickets tens of thousands of people in just a few days. (An undertaking even more impressive when one considers that the jay-walkers frequently fight back and the police estimate they need three to four officers to subdue one unruly jay-walker.) Sometimes the campaigns are effective only as campaigns—as with jay-walking—but in some cases their effect is deeper, as with the anti-smuggling campaign that was launched in 1998 and ran for several years. But the impact of a campaign in progress is unavoidable, so if it relates even peripherally to business, you had best be prepared to deal with it.

Preparedness, in fact, is another critical aspect of sinified thinking. *"Without preparedness, superiority is not real superiority and there can be no initiative either. Having grasped this point, a force which is inferior but prepared can often defeat a superior enemy by surprise attack."* The degree of preparedness required to succeed in China is high, especially if you are going to do something that will negatively impact someone else. If, for example, you plan to change your distribution system, don't let this be known until the new system is in place—should word get out beforehand, your current distributor may immediately stop distributing your product and start distributing those of your competitor, leaving you high and dry.

The same applies to firing an employee. The Donald Trump "You're fired!" approach is likely to land you in court. One multinational was sued by an employee who was fired for stealing and subsequently spent four years going through four levels of court, each of which decided against the company. In the end, the company had to pay severance to the fired employee—and then hire him back. A sinified approach to the situation would have been to demote the employee to a position such as security guard that would have caused him to quit on his own, or to plan the firing with the precision of a military campaign to ensure that it would not create more problems than it solved. One company that was determined to fire a high-level executive spent a year preparing in great secrecy. It worked with lawyers and police in every city it had business and made elaborate contingency plans for every possible move the vengeful fired employee might make to destroy the business. In a mark of true sinification, it even prepared a plan to help the disgraced employee save face once he was fired by helping him go into business for himself. As Mao said, "*Be sure to fight no battle unprepared, fight no battle you are not sure of winning; make every effort to be well prepared for each battle, make every effort to ensure victory in the given set of conditions as between the enemy and ourselves.*"

Another important aspect of sinification is self-criticism; where Westerners are taught the power of positive thinking from an early age, Chinese are taught the power of self-criticism. Self-criticism is also an important tool of Chinese Communism—Mao made others criticize themselves and was even forced to do it himself—and the current leadership continues to use it as a means of disciplining Party members, ordinary citizens, and even foreign guests. (I've been obliged to write two self-criticisms so far, and I am not very good at it.) While positive thinking can certainly bring great benefits, self-criticism is also a formidable tool.

Chinese appliance maker Haier requires employees who have made mistakes to criticize themselves in front of their colleagues at day's end, and Huawei CEO Ren Zhengfei uses Mao's theories of criticism and self-criticism during staff meetings. Multinationals that learn to practice self-criticism and make changes based upon it are likely to do better than those that focus on trumpeting their successes.

> As Mao said, *"We must not become complacent over any success. We should check our complacency and constantly criticize our shortcomings, just as we should wash our faces or sweep the floor every day to remove the dirt and keep them clean."*

If sinification is more challenging then you expect, don't despair. Having been on the receiving end of outside dogmatisms for several centuries now, China has come to expect dogmatic behavior from Westerners. While such behavior is hardly popular, it is tolerated with the somewhat patronizing attitude of a parent who knows his child will "grow out of it."

Indeed, one might even argue that China is dogmatic when it comes to requiring that foreigners change themselves for China. But now that the government is so intent on seeing Chinese companies "go global," Chinese executives will come up against their own dogmatisms as they enter foreign markets and cultures. They would do well to brush off their "Little Red Books" and remember Chairman Mao's advice: *I beg to advise you not to transplant Chinese experience mechanically. The experience of any foreign country can serve only for reference and must not be regarded as dogma.*

A CRYSTALLIZATION OF COLLECTIVE WISDOM

Now let's consider some practical ways to resist dogmatism, embrace sinification, and use your prowess at both to greatest advantage.

- **Go global with successful sinifications.**

  The Chinese market is so competitive and its consumers so demanding that China is increasingly
  seen as an excellent place to develop and test new
  products for the global market. Don't miss the
  opportunity to go global with successfully sinified
  products and practices and let China help you
  innovate.

- **Choose expats who are capable of sinifying.**

  A China-bound expat needs a deep understanding of
  your corporation and the technical or managerial
  expertise to do his job well. But he must also be open
  and flexible enough to adapt to China's unique culture and market and the fast pace at which its business environment changes. Companies should
  choose expats who are capable of detecting change—
  and of changing themselves.

- **Don't transplant mistakes.**

  Some multinationals establish "copy exactly" policies under which they build a plant in China that is
  identical or almost identical to one in their home
  country. The aim of such policies may be benign—
  even admirable—but the reality is that almost any
  operation can be improved upon the second time
  around. Local conditions, costs, and values also

should be taken into account. As Mao explained to those who wanted to copy exactly from the USSR:

The Soviet experience in construction is fairly complete. By complete I mean it includes the making of mistakes. No experience can be considered complete unless it includes the making of mistakes. To learn from the Soviet Union does not mean to copy everything mechanically, which is exactly what dogmatism does.

- **SINIFY YOUR PERSPECTIVE.**
Strive to see your world from a sinified viewpoint (while still maintaining your own). When one sinified company received a letter from a supplier accusing its procurement manager of corruption, for example, it immediately understood that it had finally found an honest manager; she wasn't giving kickbacks to the supplier as her predecessors had, so the unhappy supplier was trying to get her fired. The company kept its procurement manager and dropped the supplier. Sinifying your perspective increases your understanding and your range of options for dealing with a particular situation.

- **CREATE A CHINA-HEADQUARTERS RELATIONSHIP THAT WORKS FOR BOTH SIDES.**

  Many companies struggle to optimize the China-headquarters relationship. Solutions—or at least salves—to problematic relations include direct contact between China executives and their home-based superiors; the creation of a China committee that pulls in relevant executives from both sides of the ocean; and giving China-based executives more power to make daily decisions without having to report back home.

- **CHOOSE YOUR BATTLES.**

  Whether you are trying to fire an unwanted employee, battle a dishonest partner, or shut down an operation that is pirating your product, *"Fight when you know you can win. Don't fight battles you may lose!"*

- **MAKE GOOD USE OF ADVERSITY.**

  Mao believed strongly in the benefits of adversity. He wrote an essay called "To Be Attacked by the Enemy is Not a Bad Thing but a Good Thing," and in 1964 he rebuffed a Japanese visitor who apologized for Japan's invasion of China by explaining his view that if Japan had not attacked China, China would never have become a strong nation. *"That is why I said to him,"* Mao explained with a smile, *"Should I not thank you instead?"* Adversity is inevitable in China business, but if you are prepared to learn from your mistakes and problems, you will end up stronger for it.

- **IF IT AIN'T BROKE, DON'T FIX IT.**
Not every dogma is bad, not every imported product or practice needs sinifying. This is especially true with products and services perceived as high status or high value, or for which foreignness is part of the attraction.

- **ANTICIPATE REVENGE.**
Mao preached forgiveness, but he sought revenge. *"If people don't attack me, I won't attack them. If people attack me, I will certainly attack them. They attack me first, I attack them later. This principle I have never abandoned down to the present time. Now I have learnt to listen, to toughen my scalp and listen for one or two weeks and then counter-attack."* The Maoist culture of revenge still thrives in China, and you must prepare for its possibility even in ordinary business transactions.

- **DON'T OVERESTIMATE YOUR OWN IMPORTANCE.**
Always remember that domestic issues matter much more to the Communist Party than international business or diplomacy. As Mao once put it, *"...our basic concern is with internal problems. If we don't deal effectively*

with our internal problems, there's no good talking about international affairs." Neither your business nor your nation is as important to China as you may think it is.

- **READ THE NEWSPAPERS.**
Mao estimated that during his years as a student, a third of all his expenditures went to buying newspapers:

> *My father cursed me for this extravagance. He called it wasted money on wasted paper. But I had acquired the newspaper-reading habit, and from 1911 to 1927, when I climbed up Jinggangshan, I never stopped reading the daily papers of Peking, Shanghai, and Hunan.*

Mao's newspaper habit was instrumental in building his remarkable political perceptiveness—and it will certainly help you to build yours. (This is true even if you can only read English publications or translations. Indeed, Mao also noted that "*It takes much less time to read translations than to read the originals; therefore one can learn more in less time.*")

- **MAKE SURE YOUR CONSULTANTS ARE SINIFIED.**
Many companies complain about un-sinified consultants who, for instance, make key projections based on other markets and overlook the ways in

which China is different. If you are going to pay good money to a consultancy, make sure it is at least as sinfied as you.

- **LEARN FROM SUCCESSFUL CHINESE COMPANIES.**
Chinese companies are increasingly successful both at home and abroad, and wise foreign investors will watch and learn from them.

- **STAY ATOP CHINA'S CHANGING ECONOMIC GEOGRAPHY.**
The number of people living in cities rose from 170 million to 540 million between 1978 and 2004—and another 200 million people are expected to become urban residents by 2010. And, between 2001 and 2005, China increased the length of its expressways by 15,350 miles; it is now second only to the U.S. in interstate highway by miles and should pass it by 2020. The changing face of China's economic geography means that once inaccessible markets can now be tapped—and they must be—to stay abreast of the competition.

- **ALIGN YOURSELF WITH REGIONAL DEVELOPMENT GOALS.**
The Chinese government is eager to channel investment to up-and-coming regions. It has clear goals

and wish lists for different regions, and aligning yourself with these will make your work much easier. Moving into second- and third-tier markets also will help you cut costs, gain competitive advantages, open new markets, and lessen the impact of China's increasing economic nationalism.

NOTES

Those who regard Marxism-Leninism as religious—in Short, 381.

a form of sabotage—in Short, p. 248.

very serious mistake—in Short, p. 293.

The political appraisal and military strategy—"Some Experiences in Our Party History," 1956.

chief mistake and *transplanting foreign experience mechanically*—"Some Experiences in Our Party's History," September 25, 1956.

Whoever wants to know a thing has no way—"On Practice," 1937.

Foreign stereotypes must be abolished—"Oppose Stereotyped Party Writing," 1942.

a bunch of zombies with a slave—Li Zhisui, p. 234.

Marxism didn't just drop from heaven—Li Zhisui, p. 234.

We have launched many large-scale movements in recent—Deng Xiaoping, "Speech Delivered at an Enlarged Conference of the Party Central Committee," February 6, 1962.

More than 40 billion volumes of his—Barme, *Shades of Mao*, p. 9.

Trade with China will promote freedom—George Bush, speech at Boeing plant, May 17, 2000 (on issues2002.org).

We must plant our backsides on the body—in Short, p. 381.

The Chinese keep saying that we need—Rahul Jacob, "Joint Ventures Struggle to bridge Cultural Divide," *The Financial Times*, March 27, 2001.

There are two principles here—"The United Front in Cultural Work," October 30, 1944.

You can produce some things which are neither—"Mao's Talk to Music Workers," 1956.

Some people...say that it is enough merely to study—"Problems of Strategy in China's Revolutionary War," December 1936.

China's problems are complicated—"On the Chongqing Negotiations," October 17, 1945.

that of a war of maneuver—"On Guerrilla Warfare," 1937.

How can [anything be resolved]—in Short, p. 480.

tottering along like a woman with bound feet—in Solomon, p. 261.

Without preparedness superiority is not real—"On Protracted War," May 1938.

be sure to fight no battle unprepared—"The Present Situation and Our Tasks," December 25, 1947.

We must not become complacent over—"Get Organized!" November 29, 1943.

I beg to advise you not to transplant—"Some Experiences in Our Party's History," September 25, 1956.

The Soviet experience in construction is fairly—"Be Activists for the Revolution," 1957.

To separate internationalist content—"Oppose Stereotyped Party Writing," February 8, 1942.

Fight when you know you can win—in Short, p. 360.

That is why I said to him—in Pye, p. 62.

If people don't attack me, I won't—"Strategy for the Second Year of the War of Liberation," 1947.

Our basic concern is with internal problems—"Remarks at the Spring Festival," February 13, 1964. (In "Long Live Mao Zedong Though," a Red Guard Publication.)

My father cursed me for this extravagance—in Snow, p. 150.

It takes much less time to read—"Letter to Zhou Shizhao," 1920, in *Road to Power*, Volume I, p. 520.

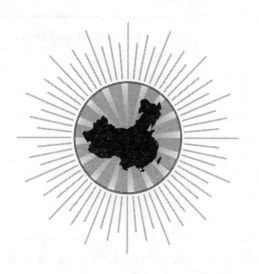

CHAPTER SEVEN

PEOPLE ARE THE
DECISIVE FACTOR

Weapons are an important factor in war, but not the decisive factor; it is people, not things, that are decisive.

This is one of Mao's most famous quotations—I read it every morning as I get dressed, since it is stenciled in gold on a Cultural Revolution-era wardrobe that I bought in Shanghai a few years back. Today, as in Mao's time, success in China hinges on the talent and dedication of the people you attract to work with you and on your ability to motivate, train, and retain them.

People Power

Mao's faith in people as the decisive factor was forged in the crucible of warfare. He saw the overthrow of the Qing Dynasty by Sun Yat-sen, the triumph of the Chinese over the Japanese in World War II, and the defeat of the Nationalists by the Communists as proof that *"small forces linked with the people become strong, while big forces opposed to the people become weak."* It was in this context that he famously called U.S. imperialism a *"paper tiger"* because *"it is divorced from the masses of the people and is disliked by everybody and by the American people too."* He also believed—as do many of his countrymen—that the Japanese were not defeated by the atom bomb, but by the Chinese masses.

So strongly did Mao believe that people are the motivating force in history that he spent much of his career effectively serving as a human resources manager. In the startup phase of the Communist Party, much of his work naturally involved recruitment. He organized laborers and worked with the peasant associations that so altered his perspective on the future course of revolution. At Stalin's insistence, the Nationalists and the Communists formed a "united front" in 1924. (Stalin believed that joining forces was the only way to defeat the warlords and create a unified China—one which he presumed would be friendly to him.) Mao joined the Nationalist Party in support of the united front, and his expertise on rural affairs helped him land an important job as acting head of the Nationalist Party Propaganda Department in 1925.

But in the spring of 1927, Chiang Kai-shek betrayed his united front allies—and Stalin—when he ordered the massacre of hundreds of Communists in Shanghai. In the terror that followed, tens of thousands of Communists and suspected Communists were arrested and shot in other cities and the united front came to an end. That autumn, Mao was ordered by the Party's Central Committee to lead a province-wide uprising in Hunan. Mao had misgivings about the plan and launched only a small uprising aimed at the provincial capital of Changsha, but even this failed. The situation went from bad to worse when Mao himself was captured and marched off to a militia headquarters for execution. Just short of their destination, Mao managed to break free from his captors, hide in tall grasses until nightfall, and then walk shoeless through the mountains to safety. With nowhere else to go—and the Communist Party itself struggling to survive—Mao led his rag-tag army into the mountains of Jiangxi Province and set about regrouping.

The soldiers in Mao's little army were not crack troops. On the contrary, they were mainly illiterate peasants, former Nationalists, and local bandits; weapons were in such short supply that many carried only spears or clubs. Joining the military had never been viewed as an honorable career choice; as the saying went "you don't turn good metal into nails, and you don't turn good men into soldiers."

Fierce, if intermittent, warfare had torn the country for decades, and it was so difficult to find men willing to enlist that the Nationalist army "recruited" by kidnapping civilian men of all ages, chaining them together, and marching them off to training camps without food or water. It has been estimated that millions of Nationalist soldiers died just in the process of being conscripted. Soldiers who were treated worse than animals tended to have little respect for civilian populations in enemy areas. The Nationalist troops were known for such tactics as "draining the pond to catch the fish" which meant they killed the men, took the grain, burned the village and sold the women and girls into prostitution. In one Hubei county, more than 100,000 villagers were slaughtered by Nationalist soldiers.

Given this challenging external environment, Mao knew that as the leader of a poorly equipped rebel army, he needed to take radical measures just to survive. So he focused on the only resource he had: people. First he announced that the army would be converted to an all-volunteer force; any soldier who wanted to leave would be given money for his travels. Soldiers who stayed would be treated with respect. They could form committees to protect their own interests, and officers would not be allowed to beat them. In turn, they would be required to treat civilian populations with courtesy and civility.

To ensure that this concept was clear, Mao created a binding code of conduct for officers and soldiers alike. The code, which covered basic points like following orders and not taking "a single needle or piece of thread from the masses," was eventually popularized as the "Three Main Rules of Discipline" and "Eight Main Points for Attention." It was used to orient all new recruits and even set to music; later, it became a staple scene in war movies, and many people can sing it to this day. Mao's new human resources policies eventually became effective recruiting tools, and his code of conduct earned the vital support of villagers in the areas through which his army passed.

Training and development were also an essential part of his survival effort, especially after his forces merged with those of the Communist General Zhu De. Since the soldiers were for the most part illiterate, Mao adapted his style of speech. He began using pithy aphorisms and folksy phrases to convey military strategy (some of which seems adapted from the work of the ancient strategist Sun Tzu.) *"The God of Thunder strikes the beancurd"* was his way of explaining the need to concentrate forces and attack the enemy's weak points. He and Zhu De also came up with a ditty to summarize their strategy of guerilla warfare: *"The enemy advances, we retreat; the enemy camps, we harass; the enemy tires, we attack; the enemy retreats, we pursue."* As the size of his army grew over the next few years, Mao also began literacy campaigns and established a promotion and review system for officers.

Staffing the Communist Party itself was even more complicated than filling the ranks of the army. The Party needed intellectuals, not footsoldiers, and it had little to offer them in the way of pay or job security. But what it did have was an *"ism."* *"An ism is like a banner,"* Mao wrote in 1920. *"Only when it is raised will the people have something to hope for and know in which direction to go."* The desire for an *"ism"* that gave hope and direction was one of the things that initially attracted Mao to Communism. The *"ism"* in Communism, and the compelling vision for a new China offered by the Party, proved an invaluable recruiting tool; not incidentally, it was a tool the Nationalists could never fully exploit.

Once the Party settled into its semi-permanent base at Yanan in 1936, it began to recruit idealistic students and intellectuals from around the country. These newcomers often were shocked when they arrived—Yanan had a magical reputation as the nerve center of the Communist cause, yet in reality, it was a poor mountainous village so isolated it could be reached only by mule train or airplane. But Mao and his colleagues established no-nonsense orientation programs aimed to make *"every comrade...sound and our entire ranks...truly united and consolidated ideologically and organizationally."*

> *"[You] have passed not only from one kind of place to another but from one historical epoch to another..."* Mao bluntly told newly arrived artists and writers from the garrets of Shanghai. *"To come to the revolutionary bases means to enter an epoch unprecedented in the thousands of years of Chinese history, an epoch in which the masses of the people wield state power. Here the people around us and the audience for our propaganda are totally different. The past epoch is gone, never to return."*

To retain the new recruits, the Party promised an easy path to membership and free higher education (including room and board) at such newly founded institutions as the Central Party School, Resist Japan Military and Political University, and the Lu Xun Academy for Literature and Arts. It created a work environment that is now the stuff of legend, with Saturday night dances for the leadership and opera under the stars for everyone. At Zhou Enlai's instruction, a symphony orchestra was even founded; its musicians were peasant youth who had never heard a violin, but a conservatory trained Communist conductor managed to teach them everything from piccolo to tuba, and eventually they were playing Schubert and Mozart (roughly).

Mao also understood that the many new recruits to the Communist cause were looking for leadership and a role model. Although he had led soldiers for some years, he was not a natural born leader. Indeed, he himself said, "*There is no such thing in the world as a 'natural leader.'*" But he became one. Making a virtue out of necessity, he insisted that everyone keep to a "*style of plain living and hard struggle*" and did so himself. He lived in a two-room cave dwelling, its walls covered with maps, and worked until the middle of the night. He was oblivious to personal appearance—Edgar Snow recounted him turning down his trousers to scratch for lice during an interview—and owned only blankets, two cotton uniforms, and a few personal belongings. He ate the same food as everyone else, except that his was laced with peppers, and his only apparent perk was the cigarettes to which he was addicted throughout his life. Snow described the effect of Mao's leadership style in the late 1930s:

The influence of Mao Zedong throughout the

Communist world of China was probably greater than that of anyone else...Yet while everyone knew and respected him, there was— as yet, at least—no ritual of hero worship built up around him...I never met one who did not like "the Chairman"—as everyone called him— and admire him. The role of his personality in the movement was clearly immense.

As the size of his organization grew and the possibility of victory became more real, Mao began to concentrate on teaching other Party members how to be effective leaders. He also put in place a succession plan with Liu Shaoqi as his anointed number two. On two occasions when Mao personally faced danger, he made arrangements for Liu to take over should the worst come to pass. (Liu was arrested during the Cultural Revolution and died in prison of medical neglect.)

CULTURAL QUIRKS

Every business culture has its own quirks. Two of those which foreigners tend to find especially odd can be traced directly to Mao: sleeping and sickness.

Meetings are a major part of Communism. In the early years of liberation, the amount of time that virtually everyone was required to spend in meetings led to the saying, "Under the Nationalist Party, there were many taxes; under the Communists, there are many meetings." While Mao recognized the importance of meetings in unifying and educating Party members and the masses at large, he also realized that to attend them was not always a scintillating experience and offered some advice for coping:

> *Rather than keeping your eyes open and listening to boring lectures, it is better to get some refreshing sleep. You don't have to listen to nonsense, you can rest your brain instead.*

Sleeping during meetings, lectures, or classes remains a fairly common practice—one that is discomfiting to foreigners, but which leaves most Chinese nonplussed. If you catch an employee sleeping during a meeting and are bothered by it, talk to him in private—singling someone out for public censure will embarrass everyone and make you seem insensitive.

If sleep is an escape from boredom, sickness is a tool for negotiation and for extricating oneself from an awkward situation or undesired task. Mao regularly took sick leave at difficult points in his revolutionary career. While the illnesses may well have been genuine—he called them *"mental ailments"*—the causes were certainly work-related and were even referred to by others as "diplomatic disorders."

Claiming sickness is still a common avoidance technique and may even include checking into the hospital. (Hospitals are viewed as retreats of a sort and checking in and out of them at will—or staying in them for months on end, but leaving for meetings and parties—remains established practice among certain sectors of society, particularly retired high-level cadres and others with sufficient means.) So, if you have an altercation with a staff member and the next day he ends up hospitalized, you may want to consider the nature of his disorder and the extent to which your disagreement has harmed your working relationship.

But even as Mao was coming into his own as a people manager—not to mention a Communist and military leader—the fundamental character flaws that would mark his future leadership of the People's Republic were starting to assert themselves. Indeed, although Mao had once rejected Marxism as too violent and had previously spoken against *"war and bloody revolutions,"* by 1927 he had changed his mind and declared *"political power grows out of the barrel of a gun."*

While he was no doubt right that the Communist Party would gain power only through military means, this realization also marked the beginning of his ever-escalating tolerance for violence in the name of politics. His intolerance for Party members who didn't agree with him also began to grow, and it would soon lead to violent rectifications and bloody purges that only grew worse as the years went by. Mao began to manipulate people rather than manage them; indeed, it almost seems that he began to think of people *as* weapons, turning them against each other like so many guns or cannons. In his later years, he stunned more than one listener with his easy talk of the human losses his nation could sustain in the face of the atom bomb. *"The United States cannot annihilate the Chinese nation with its small stack of atom bombs,"* Mao glibly told a Finnish envoy:

> *Even if the U.S. atom bombs were so powerful that, when dropped on China, they would make a hole right through the earth, or even blow it up, that would hardly mean anything to the universe as a whole, though it might be a major event for the solar system.*

The HR Challenge

Why and how Mao changed is a question that none of us can answer. But his basic people-centered approach nonetheless remains valid: people are the decisive factor. Indeed, the quote that begins this chapter should be stenciled in gold in the entryway of every multinational in China, just as it is on my wardrobe. But, the word *"war"* should be replaced with "business" and *"weapons"* with a term relevant to each organization, like technology or capital:

224

> [Technology] *is an important factor in* [business],
> *but not the decisive factor; it is people, not things,*
> *that are decisive.*

China-based executives tend to learn this the hard way. Indeed, many profess shock over the amount of time that must be dedicated to human resources related issues. They also frequently cite management-level human resources as a top challenge of doing business in China. Dispiritingly, surveys also reveal that attracting, developing, and retaining top talent does not get easier with experience—even companies who have been in China for more than twenty years say it is a major issue.

That human resources should be a top problem for foreign companies in China might sound odd to the uninitiated—it is, after all, the world's most populous nation. It has also recently become the country with the greatest number of university students—23 million in 2006. And, Chinese people are known the world over for their hard work, respect for education, and entrepreneurial drive.

To be sure, most multinationals don't complain of a dearth of unskilled factory workers. (Although there is talk of a growing shortage of skilled blue collar workers nationwide and even of unskilled workers in such dynamic growth areas as Guangdong.) But when it comes to filling professional positions—especially mid- to senior-level managers—the complaints are legion. On the one hand, multinationals have great difficulty finding staff they consider qualified, even for support positions; a 2005 report by the McKinsey Global Institute indicated that fewer than 10 percent of Chinese college graduates were considered suitable to work in a foreign company. And on the other hand, they are unable to retain the employees they do hire. One survey indicated that turnover increased from 8 percent in 2000 to 14 percent in 2005. Another revealed that the average tenure for professionals in the twenty-five to thirty-five age range is now only one to two years, as compared to three to five years in 2004. Turnover rates in certain sectors and job categories can run well above 20 percent. Unsurprisingly, many companies say their businesses are negatively affected by the difficulty in recruiting and retaining employees.

The laundry list of reasons given for the apparent dearth of qualified candidates includes insufficient English ability, leadership skills, management skills, teamwork ability, willingness to take risks, initiative, and creativity, as well as inflated salary expectations and plain old lack of experience. Historic factors are also cited, especially the enduring impact of the Cultural Revolution and the state-owned enterprise system, both of which are essentially seen to have ruined the generation of people who would normally be senior managers. When it comes to analyzing why turnover rates are so high, the reasons cited include the employees' desire for better compensation, career development opportunities, benefits, training programs, or opportunities for overseas assignments. Cultural factors such as an alleged get rich quick mentality and low sense of loyalty are also named.

Unsurprisingly, the shortage of people perceived as qualified and the high turnover rate combine to make recruitment a cutthroat endeavor, with multinationals—and an increasing number of Chinese companies—fishing from the same small pool of people. Companies actively poach from each other, and headhunters do a booming business. Chinese who have studied and worked overseas—colloquially known as sea turtles—are also a popular recruitment target.

The easiest way to resolve this problem would be to expand the pool of potential candidates. Because China's talent pool is not really small—it is just perceived as small by multinationals that are essentially looking for clones. China is full of talented, capable, and ambitious people who don't quite fit the required multinational profile; their English is rocky, their talent is raw, their experience is in a planned system, they are uncomfortable with backslapping camaraderie, and they require more training than multinationals want to give. Many China-based executives know this—and also know that they are making life difficult for themselves by fighting over the same people. But for a variety of reasons—peer pressure, competitive instincts, habit, self-protection, the difficulty of dealing with un-sinified headquarters—they do it anyway. Had Mao adopted employment standards as high and narrow as those of multinational corporations in China, it seems fair to say that he never would have won the revolution—indeed, he would never have mustered an army to join the battle.

If widening the pool of potential recruits is the best way to address recruitment problems, another is to differentiate your company from the competition. One of the best tools of differentiation is reputation. If you are a global company that is already seen to be at the top of your industry, recruitment will be much easier; if you are not, you must do more work to stand out. Some companies multitask by considering recruitment needs when they formulate marketing campaigns and do brand building. Others smartly package and promote their human resource policies rather like Mao did. This is especially effective in competition with Chinese companies, since multinationals are generally considered to have a more transparent and less hierarchical work environment that is attractive to many people. College recruitment programs are also an effective long-term recruitment tool; some corporations assign a university each to key executives and make them responsible for building relationships and developing a recruitment program.

Use Cadres Well

If recruiting talented employees is a battle, retaining them is a protracted war. The effort to keep the people you've hired should begin on their first day of work. It should include a thorough and compelling orientation program that delves into your corporation's history, culture, code of conduct, mission, and vision for the future. It should strive to make each employee believe that he has a meaningful role in an important organization. A clearly defined "ism" that lets people see how their work contributes to the greater good is of tremendous use. It is common to assume that the turnover rate in China is all about money, and that foreign corporations are viewed as ATM machines; when one reaches its cash limit, you go to another. But the reality is that people are often willing to work below the top end of the pay scale if they believe they and their company are making a unique contribution in a particular field and benefiting China. Remember how excited Mao Zedong got about making soap?

A clear path for career development is also a crucial element of retention. Many of the young idealists who went to Yanan stayed on because they were allowed to join the Party. The "Party" that runs your corporation must be open to all; if there is a glass ceiling blocking the promotion of Chinese nationals, you will have retention problems. Career development should be concrete, rather than vague, and it should include regular progress checks, performance reviews, mentoring relationships, and even professional career counseling. Many young people know only the state-owned enterprise model of their parent's generation or the job-hopping model of this generation; they do not understand the benefits of building a stable career with a single organization.

Training is a key element in career development. Just as China wants to learn foreign things to develop Chinese things, so do individual Chinese want to develop themselves by working for multinationals. But to serve as a retention tool, training must be offered in stages and delivered as promised. It must also be clearly integrated with business goals so participants understand that the training is not an end in itself; misunderstandings often occur when an employee completes one training and wants to move right on to the next, causing resentment among managers who first want to see the results applied to work. Training should also occur informally through interaction with managers—and this means that teaching should be part of every manager's job description, and teaching effectiveness should be a part of his evaluation.

A positive and fun work environment also can help keep employees happy and loyal. Chinese companies are often run something like families; they are frequently dysfunctional, but they retain loyalty through the shared bonds of people who together work long hours, play badminton and ping-pong on breaks, and enjoy company funded weekends away (without spouses or children). In this "family" environment, the role of the manager is crucial—it is his relationship to each employee that drives loyalty. A manager is often expected to listen to personal problems, inquire after sick relatives, know the names of family members, and play a more personal mentoring role than in Western organizations. Mao was always at those Saturday night fiestas in Yanan, although he sat out most dances because people wanted to chat with him. As he noted, *"If a bow-string is too taut, it will snap. The ancients said, 'The principle of Kings Wen and Wu was to alternate tension with relaxation.' Now 'relax' a bit and the comrades will become more clear-headed."*

Another crucial factor in retention is each individual's relationship with his superior; as is often said, employees join organizations, but leave bosses. Leadership must be displayed at every level—especially the top. Good leaders must give their subordinates real responsibility and the authority to exercise it. Because the fear of making a mistake runs high in China, employees must be repeatedly encouraged to express opinions, share ideas, and take risks. *"We must create an environment in which people will dare to speak out and reveal what is in their hearts."* If they make a mistake, they should not be punished and should be given the chance to try again—and other employees should know of this. As Mao also said (but certainly did not always practice), *"For comrades who have*

*committed mistakes, the policy of 'learning from past mistakes
to avoid future ones' and 'curing the illness to save the patient'
should be adopted."*

Since so much is expected of executives—teaching,
mentoring, relationship building, dealing with headquarters, running a business, and so forth—it is vital to make
sure that they get the support they need from back home.
If they are local Chinese, this means making it clear that
they are valued and trusted members of your corporation,
and not just of your China business; integrating them into
the company globally so they are a known quantity at
headquarters and can get the resources and support they
need; and providing them with any training or education
that might better enable them to do their jobs, and
encourage them to stay on. If they are expatriates, they
will presumably already have strong connections at home,
but they will still need support in maintaining these as
executives back home change. They also need to be given
the training, resources, and support they need to do their
jobs in China; given their cost to the company and the
high expectations placed on them, it is surprising how little China-related training expatriate executives actually
receive.

People are the ultimate secret to your success in
China. *"We must know how to use cadres well. In the final
analysis, leadership involves two main responsibilities: to work
out ideas, and to use cadres well."*

BLANK PAPER

Mao, like all writers, liked blank paper.

On a blank sheet of paper free from any mark, the freshest and most beautiful characters can be written, the freshest and most beautiful pictures can be painted.

He also liked blank humans.

From ancient times the people who have created new schools of thought have always been young people without great learning. Confucius started at the age of twenty-three; and how much learning did Jesus have?...The inventor of sleeping pills was not even a doctor, let alone a famous doctor; he was only a pharmacist...Franklin of America, who discovered electricity, began as a newspaper boy.

(When Mao got old himself, his admiration for youth and emptiness took on a physical dimension and he began to bed a succession of uneducated young women, but that's another story.)

Mao's appreciation for blankness is shared by those China-based executives who prefer to employ young, malleable people who speak good English but have little experience. This approach does make some sense—if you hire people who are not quite up to the job, they will be challenged and will learn and thus feel fulfilled and be more likely to stay with your company.

But, some executives argue it has been taken too far. It narrows the pool of prospective employees and leaves multinationals to compete for the same group of English-speaking college graduates. Since the only experience that is valued is that in other multinationals, it encourages poaching and contributes to low retention rates. More importantly, it excludes vast numbers of people whose experience in the state system might well be relevant to your business—a government relations manager needs to understand and have connections in the Chinese government, while a procurement manager must be able to navigate a complex and corrupt network of suppliers. Good English and an eagerness to learn is simply not enough for some jobs—experience does count.

A CRYSTALLIZATION OF COLLECTIVE WISDOM

Now let's consider some practical tips for attracting and retaining high-performing people.

- **REMEMBER THAT BOTH TREES AND PEOPLE TAKE TIME TO GROW.**

There is an old Chinese saying you hear a lot at human resources conferences in China: "It takes ten years to grow trees but a hundred years to rear people." Mao Zedong once repeated this proverb only to challenge it by noting that trees often need much longer to grow, while people can be grown much more quickly. Unfortunately, Mao's attitude is shared by many foreign companies who expect their local managers to grow much faster than is generally possible. While it may be technically true that people grow faster than trees, rushing the process only leads to disappointment on all sides.

- **FORM A WISDOM COMMITTEE.**

When high-level Communist Party leaders retire, they reportedly join a Wisdom Committee which provides advice to their successors. The problems with such a committee are obvious—the advice may not always be solicited or welcomed—but the idea is a good one that multinationals would do well to emulate. The wisdom of repatriated, or even retired, executives with China experience should be channeled to productive purpose instead of wasted as is so often the case. Former China executives could advise their replacements, participate in strategy sessions, or simply become part of a database that current China-based executives can access if they choose.

- **FIGHT THE "ME FIRST" TENDENCY—IN YOURSELF AS WELL AS IN OTHERS.**

  "What are these people after?" Mao asked of cadres who displayed what he called "me first" tendencies. *"They are after fame and position and want to be in the limelight. Whenever they are put in charge of a branch of work, they assert their 'independence.' With this aim, they draw some people in, push others out and resort to boasting, flattery and touting among the comrades . . ."* This is a sentiment that you sometimes hear echoed by headquarters executives who find their China-based colleagues hard to work with. If you are a China-based executive, try to understand the home office perspective—keep them informed, share the limelight, and resist the desire to think *"me first."*

- **AVOID "CLOSED-DOORISM" WHICH "JUST 'DRIVES THE FISH INTO DEEP WATERS AND THE SPARROWS INTO THE THICKETS...'"**

  Closed-doorism—closing your door to avoid problems or the necessity of listening to other people's ideas—is more common than you might think, especially in troubled businesses. In some companies, it is a special problem for Chinese managers and employees, who complain that their expatriate colleagues do not listen to them. Instead of closing your door and your ears, follow the advice which Mao gave (but himself frequently ignored): *"...Create an environment in which people will dare to speak out and reveal what is in their hearts"* and *"...Since people have mouths, let them speak. You must listen to the other person's point of view...I know it's not easy."*

- **BE VIGILANT ABOUT COMMUNICATION.**

  Corporate communication is a problem worldwide, but it can be especially challenging when language and cultural differences come into play. But this does not mean communication should be avoided, only that you must work harder at it. Because, *"Once the masses know the truth and have a common aim, they will work together with one heart. This is like fighting a battle; to win a battle the fighters as well as the officers must be of one heart."*

- **REMEMBER TO INCLUDE ALL HR COSTS WHEN YOU BUDGET.**

  Managing your human resources in China is not only time-consuming but also costly. The reality is that many executives—not just those in the HR function—will be obliged to devote considerable time and energy to recruitment, retention, and training. You would do well to budget for these activities not only in the startup phase, but throughout the life of your business venture.

- **MOVE BEYOND LANGUAGE SKILLS.**

  Consider the real importance of fluent English in job requirements. Odds are you'll find that people can be very good at their jobs without speaking fluent English—just like you can be good at your job without speaking fluent Chinese. This is especially true if your business, or the job function, is primarily focused on the domestic market.

- **GLOBALIZE YOUR HUMAN RESOURCES.**

  To globalize your employees, you must give them the same chances to develop and excel within your corporation as your employees outside China. Chinese employees should be treated as global employees of your corporation, not as local employees of your China division. Globalizing your local employees is the counterpart to sinifying your company and yourself; if you do both, you will achieve a healthy unity of opposites.

- **THINK TWICE ABOUT USING HANDCUFFS.**

  Some companies attempt to retain employees by using golden handcuffs such as stock options, cars, and housing allowances, or iron handcuffs, like penalties for early departure or stringent non-competition clauses. But, as Mao understood (but Chiang Kai-shek did not), handcuffed soldiers do not make good fighters. Mao stuck with this philosophy at what was arguably the tensest moment of his post-1949 career, the aborted 1971 coup attempt by his designated successor Lin Biao. Lin—who created "The Little Red Book" and obsequiously fanned the flames of Mao worship—fled in an aircraft which Zhou Enlai suggested be shot down with a missile. Mao replied, *"Rain will fall from the skies. Widows will remarry. What can we do? Lin Biao wants to flee. Let him. Don't shoot."* (During Lin's escape flight, Mao was taken to the Great Hall of the People and put under the highest level security; he passed the time reading history books until word came that Lin's plane had crashed in Mongolia of its own accord.)

- **RETAIN THROUGH INCENTIVES.**
Salary inflation is rampant at foreign-invested enterprises but has done little to solve the retention problem. Escape the cycle by giving incentive pay a greater role in compensation packages. Pay-for-performance is likely to appeal to the sort of employee you wish to retain and is also a classic example of mutual benefit.

- **"ALWAYS KEEP TO THE STYLE OF PLAIN LIVING AND HARD STRUGGLE."**
OK, so the "plain living" part of Mao's exhortation is unlikely to attract most expatriate executives. But if your living isn't plain, at the very least make sure that

your hard struggle matches that of your Chinese colleagues and employees—don't expect them to work all night while you go home for dinner at 6:00, demand hardship allowances as part of your package, and take regular R&Rs in Thailand.

- **HIRE PEOPLE WHOSE VALUES ARE ALIGNED WITH YOUR CORPORATE PHILOSOPHY.**
  China's fast-growing market and rapid employee turnover may make companies feel pressured to hire quickly. But taking the time to hire people whose values match your corporation's will save you trouble down the road. Mao understood this—look how he managed to retain the loyalty of the urbane and sophisticated Zhou Enlai, who seems to have deplored Mao's excesses but who remained loyal in service of the higher cause of Communism. The Communist Party also understands this—that's why it is so selective in admitting people and spends so much time immersing them in Communist values training after they are admitted. Choosing people with shared values will also help with retention—whether they are new hires or your already valued employees who will find more satisfaction in working with the newcomers.

- **"THERE IS NO SUCH THING IN THE WORLD AS A 'NATURAL LEADER.'"**
  Expatriate managers are often expected to take on many more responsibilities than they would at home and to play a major role in recruitment, retention, and training, all of which require inspired leadership. Chinese executives, too, are often expected to demonstrate Western-style leadership skills with which they are culturally unfamiliar. It is therefore wise to consider leadership potential when selecting executives, make leadership training readily available (or even require it), and to be patient in grooming your future leaders.

- **PREPARE FOR DEPARTURES.**
  No matter how hard you try to retain people, some of your valued employees will leave. Be prepared for this by ensuring that you have built in systems that will keep their knowledge and connections in your company after they leave. This is not easy—knowledge and connections are power, and people like to hold them close—but it is crucial. Likewise, it is wise to find ways to cooperate with those of your employees who are leaving to fulfill the China dream of starting their own business.

- **BE SURE TO REINFORCE THE BEHAVIORS YOU SAY YOU WANT.**

  Mao wanted Party members to dare, rather than obey; to be active rather than passive; to accept responsibility rather than pass it on; to be bold rather than fear mistakes; to speak honestly rather than ingratiatingly—or at least he said he did. In reality, he promoted sycophants and purged truth-tellers, crushed initiatives that did not originate with him, and generally demanded absolute subservience to his will. Don't make his mistake—if you say you want people to speak up, to make mistakes, to challenge the status quo, be sure to reinforce this behavior and do it in a very public way.

Notes:

Weapons are an important factor in war—"On Protracted War," May 1958.

small forces linked with the people become—"U.S. Imperialism is a Paper Tiger," 1956.

paper tiger" and "*it is divorced from the masses*—"U.S. Imperialism is a Paper Tiger," 1956.

The God of Thunder strikes the beancurd—Short, p. 214.

The enemy advances, we retreat—"A Single Spark Can Start a Prairie Fire," January 5, 1930.

An ism is like a banner—"Letter to his friend Luo Zhanglong," November 1920, in *Road to Power*, Volume I, p. 110.

every comrade...sound and our entire ranks—"Talks at Yanan Forum on Literature and Arts," 1942.

There is no such thing in the world as a "natural leader"—"The Truth About U.S. Mediation and the Civil War in China," September 29, 1946.

style of plain living and hard struggle—"Persevere in Plain Living and Hard Struggle, Maintain Close Ties with the Masses," March 1957.

The influence of Mao Zedong throughout the—Snow, p. 92.

Rather than keeping your eyes open—in Feigon, p. 147.

mental ailments—in Short, p. 361.

diplomatic disorders—in Short, p. 313.

war and bloody revolutions—in Spence, Mao, p. 50.

political power grows out of the barrel of a gun—"Problems of War and Strategy," November 6, 1938.

The United States cannot annihilate the Chinese—"The Chinese People Cannot Be Cowed by the Atom Bomb," January 28, 1955.

Dispiritingly, surveys also reveal that attracting—see 2005 American Chamber of Commerce in China survey.

a 2005 report by the McKinsey Global Institute—"Addressing China's Looming Talent Shortage," October 2005.

One survey indicated that turnover increased from 8 percent in 2000 to 14 percent in 2005—Hewitt Associates Survey.

Another revealed that the average tenure for professionals in the twenty-five to thirty-five age—Mercer Human Resources Consulting survey.

If a bow-string is too taut, it will snap—"A Talk to the Editorial Staff of the *Shansi-Suiyuan Daily*," April 2, 1948.

We must create an environment in which—Schram, p. 122.

For comrades who have committed mistakes—"Talk at the 8th Plenary Session of the CPC 8th Central Committee," August 2, 1959.

We must know how to use cadres well—"Quotations from Chairman Mao," Chapter 29.

"On a blank sheet of paper—"Introducing a Cooperative," April 1958, Solomon, p. 343.

"From ancient times the people- "Talks at Chengdu: Against Blind Faith in Learning," Schram, pp. 118–119.

"What are these people after—"Rectify the Party's Style of Work," February 1, 1942.

Closed-doorism just 'drives the fish—"On Tactics Against Japanese Imperialism," December, 1935.

Create an environment in which people—"Talks at Chengdu: Against Blind Faith in Learning," Schram, p. 122.

Since people have mouths—"Speech at the Lushan Conference," Schram, p. 137.

Once the masses know the truth—"A Talk to the Editorial Staff of the Shaanxi-Suiyuan Daily," April 2, 1948.

Rain will fall from the skies—as quoted in Li Zhisui, p. 537.

"*Always keep to the style of plain*—"Always Keep to the Style of Plain Living and Hard Struggle," October 26, 1949.

"*There is no such thing in the world*—"The Truth About U.S. Mediation and the Civil War in China," September 29, 1946.

CHAPTER EIGHT

SERVE THE PEOPLE

We should be modest and prudent, guard against arrogance and rashness, and serve the Chinese people heart and soul...

This is another of Mao's most famous sayings. When you drive past the front gate of the Chinese leadership compound of Zhongnanhai, you will see it written in gold in Mao's own calligraphy on the screen that shields the interior of the leaders' haven from prying eyes. But however indelibly linked this slogan is to Mao, the verdict on how he ultimately served the Chinese people is still out.

SERVE THE PEOPLE, REDUX

"Serve the People" is one of the "three old essays" which were written by Mao before 1949 and subsequently memorized by virtually everyone in China. (The other two are "In Memory of Norman Bethune" and "The Foolish Old Man Who Moved Mountains.") It became a core value and unofficial slogan of the Communist Party and to this day adorns many government buildings around China. Soldiers of the People's Liberation Army still use it in ceremonial greetings:

Inspecting official: "Greetings, Comrades!"

Troops: "Greetings, Leader!"

Inspecting official: "Comrades have worked hard."

Troops: "Serving the people!"

"Serve the People" remains one of the most widely-used Maoisms in the popular vocabulary, the name of a popular Thai restaurant, a trendy Beijing disco, a banned erotic novel, and a favorite slogan to emblazon tee shirts and handbags.

Judging Mao

Tens of millions of people died during Mao's rule because of his bad decisions and deliberate purges. Millions more suffered for years because they were intellectuals or "capitalist roaders," performers of Beethoven sonatas or children of men and women who—like Mao himself—once belonged to the Nationalist Party. On the other hand, many other millions of people were lifted out of crushing poverty and servitude. They were given access to basic, life-prolonging health care and the opportunity to learn how to read. Women in particular benefited from Mao's recognition that they "*hold up half the sky*" and his insistence that they be treated equally by society and the law.

Mao's great faith in the talent of the Chinese people and the value of Chinese culture made him determined to see his nation stand up among the global community of nations. "*China has inherited a backward economy. But the Chinese people are brave and industrious...The day is not far off when China will attain prosperity. There is absolutely no ground for pessimism about China's economic resurgence.*" Mao was right, and the resurgence he dreamed of is real—although his blind insistence on class struggle, his love of chaos, and his emphasis on building the new by destroying the old made it a much longer and more painful process than anyone could have expected.

Westerners now tend to focus on Mao's crimes against his people and ignore his contributions; they equate him with Stalin, forgetting that he is also the Chinese equivalent of Lenin. The Chinese view is more complex. A minority of individuals certainly hate Mao, while another minority literally worship him in temples built in his honor. Many more profess an abiding respect for his talent and tireless efforts to build the Chinese nation, mixed with regret—strong or weak, depending on personal history and education—over his failed policies that caused so much suffering.

The official evaluation, of course, is that his service was 70 percent good and 30 percent bad, which is essentially a politically expedient way to say that the early Mao was all good and the later Mao was all bad. As his colleague Chen Yun allegedly said, "Had Mao died in 1956, his achievements would have been immortal. Had he died in 1966, he would still have been a great man. But he died in 1976. Alas, what can one say."

A CABBIE'S VIEW

China's cab drivers are among the nation's most loquacious purveyors of honest opinions, ever ready to set you straight when you think things are going well. They also tend to be big Mao supporters, fond of making such statements as "When Chairman Mao was here, we were all poor but we were equally poor, not like now!" Or, "When Mao Zedong was alive, there was no corruption! The leaders' children didn't all get rich off the country like they do now. Chairman Mao sent his oldest son to die in Korea!"

Cabbies were the most noticeable adherents of the Mao Fever of the late 1990s, which started when a cab driver in Shenzhen survived a terrible accident—allegedly because he had a portrait of Chairman Mao dangling from his rear view mirror. For many months, seemingly every cab in the country sported a similar Mao icon, and a few still do.

When I told one cab driver, a Mr. Zhang, about the subject of this book in the summer of 2006, he had this to say:

> In Chinese history, the emperor who starts the dynasty is always a man of great ability. We don't say emperor now, we say leader, but it is the same thing. Mao was a man of very special ability.
>
> When Mao was here, we had Lei Feng— people acted like Lei Feng, they were good to each other. Now everyone is selfish and after money. Look at that guy in the

BMW—he has money and he has power so he wants everyone to know it, he doesn't signal, he cuts across lanes, he drives too fast. When I see people like him, I have no hope.

What we need is a combination of Mao Zedong's thought and moral teachings, and Deng Xiaoping's reform and opening to the outside world. We need the openness and development and improving living standards, but we don't need the corruption and the crime and the selfishness. Deng Xiaoping Theory cannot compare to Mao Zedong Thought. "It doesn't matter if the cat is black or white as long as it catches the mouse." What kind of thinking is that? Is that really true? If I make money by robbing a bank, that's OK because it's money? Of course not!

And, truthfully, the violence of the Cultural Revolution is not so different from the violence of today, except now it's gangs and mafia instead of Red Guards. What's the big difference?

We need to teach Mao's thought. It isn't taught because some people hate Mao the person because they suffered under him. But Mao's thought should be taught—it is separate from the man.

> We need the second Mao Zedong. Only when we get a second Mao Zedong will China's problems get better. But he will come. You'll see—he will come.

We can only guess at what Mao would say about his service. Certainly he knew that he had not accomplished all he set out to accomplish. When President Nixon flattered him with the comment that his writings had "moved a nation and...changed the world," he responded by saying, "*I have not been able to change it. I have only been able to change a few places in the vicinity of Beijing.*" In the months before he died, he declared that he had done two things that mattered, both of them pre-1949—fought Chiang Kai-shek for years and successfully chased him off to "*that little island*" and "*asked the Japanese to return to their ancestral home*" and then fought his way into the Forbidden City. But perhaps his most revealing self-evaluation comes from his youth, when he wrote to a friend, "*I have a very great defect which I feel ashamed to reveal to others: I am weak-willed. You often say that my will is strong, but in fact I have clear self-knowledge: there is nothing weaker than my will!*"

Will, of course, is perhaps the quality for which Mao is most noted. His friend saw it in 1921 and Henry Kissinger saw it when he met Mao half a century later and wrote, "I have met no one, with the possible exception of Charles De Gaulle, who so distilled raw, concentrated will power...he

253

dominated the room—not by the pomp that in most states confers a degree of majesty on the leaders, but by exuding in almost tangible form the overwhelming drive to prevail." But Mao meant something entirely different when he called himself weak-willed.

> *I have long since learned that on earth only those who attain complete gentleness can be most firm. I myself, however, am not capable of practicing this truth, so I knowingly violate it and do exactly the opposite without hesitation. How dreadful it is to think of this! What nevertheless gives me a little consolation is that I cherish my ideal sincerely (just to have that ideal) and am responsible for what I say and what I do.*

These words, penned by Mao himself, are perhaps the greatest condemnation of his person and his rule, greater than the many heavy volumes of "unknown stories" and Cultural Revolution memoirs that weigh down bookshelves in the West. He knowingly violated what he knew to be right and he is responsible for what he said and did. But if he is responsible for the bad, he is also responsible for the good, and this is why many Chinese people can forgive him his great errors and flaws—despite everything, he did try to serve the people.

Ways to Serve

The Communist Party continues to premise its right to exclusive political power on its ability to serve the people— nowadays by enabling economic development and helping all of its citizens to become "moderately prosperous," rather than directly providing social services as it did in the Mao era. Since you are in China to serve its interests, it naturally expects you to help serve the people, too. Most foreign corporations accept this premise and—having spent years learning the ropes and struggling to gain market share—are now stable and profitable enough to make this an aspect of their business. Indeed, serving the people— also known as corporate social responsibility, or CSR—is increasingly seen not only as morally and politically correct, but as good for business. It also happens to fit in neatly with the current leadership's emphasis on more equitable wealth distribution, sustainable development, and the establishment of a harmonious society.

Serving the people takes many forms. The most basic, which many companies stressed in their first decade and more of investment, is simply the introduction of Western business practices to China. This includes a generally rigorous adherence to Chinese laws and regulations; implementation of international health, safety, labor and environmental codes; enhanced employee benefits, compensation, and training programs; the establishment of research and development centers; and the application of corporate codes of conduct and ethical business practices. Western business methods are particularly seen to have served as both an example and a competitive impetus to the improvement of product quality and customer service in China.

While this line of reasoning may sound dogmatic, if you had been in China in the 1980s, begging a waitress to bring you a chipped bowl of coarse rice which would inevitably have pebbles in it because it was threshed on the side of a road; pleading with a state-run department store saleswoman wearing a white hat, seven layers of clothing, sleeve-protectors, and a sour face to glance your way, just once, so you could buy a navy blue Mao cap; or purchasing things for strangers every time you went to the Friendship Store because Chinese people, who were not allowed to enter it, stood outside with fists of tattered money pleading with foreigners to help them acquire some batteries or shampoo, you would find it impossible to rebut.

Multinationals have long supplemented their presence in China with charitable works. These are often donations in money or kind to government operated non-government organizations (GONGOs) such as the China Youth Development Foundation's Project Hope, which builds schools in poor rural areas, or to the small but growing group of genuine Chinese and international NGOs that are active in China. Charitable works also include donations for disaster relief—like shipments of

track shoes to flooded towns or hamburgers to earth-
quake zones—and support of local cultural, educational
and charitable facilities. Charitable donations have the
benefit of being simple with a dependable public relations payback. Indeed, there is a fairly direct relationship
between a big donation (for example, $1 million in U.S.
dollars and up) to a high-profile GONGO and a meeting and photo op with a high-level leader—the bigger
the donation, the higher level the leader, and the better
the press coverage.

THE VALUE OF AN EDUCATION:

Education is one of the most popular vehicles for
corporate charitable giving because the value of education is so universally accepted in China. Even Mao
took this path—as a young Communist, he founded
a "self-study university" in Hunan which was
intended to provide affordable education to all. *"In
Chinese society today, educated people cannot do manual
labor, and laborers cannot get education,"* he wrote per-
ceptively in 1920. *"Because those who are educated do not
toil, education has almost become something that creates
hooligans. Because the laborers are not educated, an occupation has almost become something that creates slaves."*

But serving the people is more than a side effect of standard Western business practices or the making of charitable contributions. Important, necessary, high-profile, and

well-intentioned though charity may be, anyone with money can write a check. Companies that are on the ground in China can do much more—and ultimately gain much more—through active, rather than passive, service to the people. Active service to the people often starts with volunteerism—painting orphanages, tutoring school children—and moves on to organizational assistance and the establishment of a long-term relationship which may include the provision of assistance, advice, and donations. Some companies create such relationships with or through established NGOs or GONGOs, while others find their own partners in the local community or adopt schools, hospitals, and even entire villages in rural areas.

LEI FENG: THE MODEL VOLUNTEER

The synonym for "volunteer" in China is a young soldier named Lei Feng.

Lei Feng—also known as the "number one rustless screw in the revolution"—was born in Mao Zedong's home province in 1940 into rough circumstances. His father was killed by the Japanese, his mother hanged herself after being raped by their landlord, a work accident took his older brother's arm, and his younger brother starved and froze to death. The despised landlord evicted Lei Feng after a quarrel and, according to a 1963 account, the young orphan "wandered from place to place, sleeping in old neglected temples, wearing strips of tree bark for clothes, eating wild fruits, and drinking cold water. In summer, his body was covered with scars from the bites of mosquitoes and ants...But he did not shed one tear. He wanted to live and have his revenge!"

Lei Feng got his wish after liberation when he bitterly accosted the landlord at a struggle rally, wrung his neck, and witnessed his execution. (These details are generally left out of modern accounts of his life.) His thirst for revenge satisfied, Lei Feng devoted himself to serving the Communist Party. He drove a tractor for agricultural collectivization and an excavator for industrialization, and in 1960, he joined the People's Liberation Army. The PLA proved an excellent platform for a doer of good deeds. Lei Feng darned socks for his fellow soldiers; shared his lunch though hungry himself; donated much of his life's savings to a People's Commune; sent his only moon cake to an old people's home; taught math, language, and culture; studied all four volumes of Mao Zedong's *Selected Works*; and kept a journal in which he penned thoughts like "to live is to serve the people." Life was good, but it got even better the day he joined the Party in 1960 and wrote:

The great Party and wise Chairman Mao! I owe my new life to you!...Everything I have belongs to you...I will serve the people wholeheartedly...I am willing to go through a sea of fire and a mountain of knives for the cause of the Party, and for the freedom, liberation, and happiness of all mankind. I'll die for the Party. I'll never change!

Lei Feng's service to the people was cut tragically short on August 15, 1962 when a truck toppled a utility pole and killed him at age twenty-two. His two-hundred-thousand-word journal was subsequently discovered and on March 5, 1963, Mao Zedong declared that the entire nation should "Learn from Lei Feng." Lei Feng campaigns have been held periodically ever since, and March 5 is "Learn From Lei Feng" day. Images of Lei Feng—which were either found or created after his death, depending on your level of credulity—remain ubiquitous. The one I like best is of the rosy-cheeked soldier wearing a big fur hat with the ear flaps sticking out.

In 2006, new photos of a trendier Lei Feng were amazingly "discovered" and it was revealed that he actually had a sporty haircut, wore a leather jacket, rode a motorcycle in Tiananmen Square, and had a girlfriend. He also posthumously started a blog and became the subject of an online video game called "Learn From Lei Feng" in which players start by darning socks and, allied with Party secretaries against the forces of evil, progress through a series of good deeds to the ultimate reward—an autograph session with Chairman Mao.

When you actively serve the people, you will almost invariably benefit as much as those you intend to help. Active service requires you to get off that horse Mao spoke of and learn about the problems and issues of society on a far deeper level than you probably ever would—or could—in your normal work life. It unites employees and provides them with a sense of usefulness—even an "ism," as in volunteerism—that may not grow directly out of their work. It links you to other important sectors of society—the disenfranchised, the non-government or quasi-non-government sector, the bureaucracies that intersect with education, poverty, or rural areas, and the media that covers this work.

If you opt to involve your headquarters in the project, it will provide them with a new window on China and a way to feel connected to your China operations on a more personal level.

XUYI COUNTY

Even a small-scale "serve the people" program that takes minimal effort to start will pay big dividends.

Soon after I established the Shanghai office of the U.S.-China Business Council, an American colleague based in DC put me in touch with a Chinese classmate who invited me to visit Xuyi County in Jiangsu Province and I accepted the offer. Jiangsu is one of China's richest provinces and Xuyi County is only two or three hours from the provincial capital of Nanjing. But it is surrounded by mountains that isolate it and bisected by the Huai River. While the county seat seemed prosperous enough, with its paved roads and fashionable female traffic police, I was shocked by the poverty of its rural areas.

In one village—called Baota, or Precious Pagoda—I visited an elementary school that had no electricity, no heat, few books, and no toys or sports equipment of any kind. The school's sixty-one boys and thirty-seven girls sat on backless stools at rough-hewn desks in classrooms adorned only by tattered posters of the Russian writers Gorky and Lermontov. Their teachers—who then earned the equivalent of eight U.S. dollars a month—were a dedicated group, but they had little to work with.

From this single visit, a long-term relationship was born as Council employees "adopted" the Baota Village Elementary School. We collected enough money—solely from Council staff and their friends and families—to install electricity in the school and buy nearly a thousand books to start a library. In subsequent years, money was raised to give teacher bonuses, build a basketball court, and replace the ancient desks. Council staff from DC began to add the village to their itinerary on China visits, giving them a unique opportunity to get out of the booming cities and gain a sense of what life was still like for hundreds of millions of rural people.

> Staff who did not visit China were included by the letters, photos, and gifts that the schoolchildren sent and by the progress report prepared each year by the school principal.
>
> Thanks to the dedication of the Council's long-serving director of management and budget, Rick Peterman, this mutually beneficial relationship is still ongoing a decade later, bringing aid to a generation of Baota schoolchildren and enlightenment to a generation of U.S.-China Business Council staff.

If the public relations aspect is handled well, it can also do much to improve your company's public image, which can help with a whole range of issues, from recruitment to problem-solving to mitigating negative media or internet publicity. And, as noted earlier, if conducted on a significant scale, it can also bring you political access and nationwide press coverage. As long as you are prepared to devote sufficient resources to make your CSR program a long-term and sustainable aspect of your China business, there is no end to the mutual benefit that comes from serving the people.

PARAGON OF VIRTUE—OR PART OF THE PROBLEM?

Mao Zedong is popularly viewed in China as a paragon of incorruptibility—especially when compared to many of today's leaders. His position enriched neither his family nor himself—indeed, he told his doctor that he wanted his children to receive no special treatment, not even special dining privileges or admission to the best hospital. When his oldest daughter by Jiang Qing came under criticism during the Cultural Revolution, he did nothing to help her.

But a more cynical observer might note that Mao had little apparent incentive to be financially corrupt since everything he needed was provided free of charge. When it came to sex—something he apparently cared about a great deal—he was quite corrupt. And he was not exactly innocent of nepotism—he did, after all, let his wife become one of the most powerful leaders in the nation.

It is also perhaps simplistic to argue that China was free of corruption in the Mao era. It was largely free of financial corruption because few people had money with which to be corrupt. But there was plenty of trading of privileges and connections to get what perks were available, to avoid being sent far from home on a countryside stint, to get into university when they were reopened to the offspring of workers, peasants, and soldiers in 1973.

While Deng's "black cat, white cat" philosophy certainly contributed to the post-Mao get-rich-quick-at-any-cost mentality, so did the dearth of physical goods, the class discrimination, and the denial of opportunity that were the norm under

Mao. Even Mao's own attitude toward corruption proves mixed on closer inspection. According to his doctor, Mao cared little if the people working for him were corrupt, so long as they were loyal. He didn't mind cheating, either. Indeed, he boasted to Edgar Snow that he wrote school entrance exam essays not just for himself, but for two friends, so was *"in reality admitted three times!"*

In his later years, Mao argued that such cheating should be public policy. *"At examinations whispering into each other's ears and taking other people's places ought to be allowed. If your answer is good and I copy it, then mine should be counted as good. Whispering in other people's ears and taking examinations in other people's names used to be done secretly. Let it now be done openly. If I can't do something and you write down the answer, which I then copy, this is all right. Let's give it a try. We must do things in a lively fashion, not in a lifeless fashion."*

The "liveliness" of the China market can be attested to by anyone who has ever tried to protect intellectual property here—but not all of the blame can be laid at Deng Xiaoping's doorstep.

A CRYSTALLIZATION OF COLLECTIVE WISDOM

Here are a few tips for making sure that your service really brings benefits to the people and also supports your own goals.

- **MAKE SURE YOUR "SERVE THE PEOPLE" ENDEAVORS ARE ABOVE SUSPICION.**

  It is no secret that companies undertake to serve the people in part because they hope it will bring indirect benefits to their business. Observing this in 1923, Mao commented, *"Because they have no commercial power in Hunan, the Americans put all their energies into charitable enterprises such as raising funds for religion, education, and hospitals. The average student who goes to study in the United States consequently develops a rather strong pro-American attitude."* Be certain that your philanthropy or volunteerism is not perceived to be illegitimate in any way.

- **DEVELOP A COMPREHENSIVE SERVE THE PEOPLE— OR CSR—STRATEGY.**

  Many companies still serve the people on an ad hoc basis, donating money to a cause that catches their eye or sponsoring an event suggested by a particularly persistent caller. A better approach is to integrate your CSR activities regionally, China-wide, or even globally, and tie them to your corporate philosophy. It is also essential that CSR activities have a clear owner within your China business; some companies have even begun to create a CSR function or position to handle their "serve the people" activities. An integrated CSR strategy will ultimately serve you—and the people—best.

- **AVAIL YOURSELF OF OUTSIDE RESOURCES.**
  The growing interest in CSR has resulted in a boom in consultants, committees, companies, websites, and NGOs that provide assistance in forming and implementing CSR strategies—indeed, the Chinese government has even created a Research Center of CSR and Charity Affairs. Exchanging information with others involved in CSR is certain to bring you mutual benefit.

- **JUST SAY NO TO CORRUPTION.**
  Corruption will ultimately do you more harm than good, and it certainly doesn't serve the people. Don't practice it—and don't tolerate it.

- **MAKE SERVING THE PEOPLE A PART OF YOUR CORPORATE "ISM."**
  A strong CSR policy makes employees feel good about working for your company and—if it involves their participation—brings them together in ways that may ultimately benefit your business.

- **INVOLVE EMPLOYEES IN YOUR CSR ACTIVITIES.**

  Involving employees in your CSR activities is worth the extra effort it will take. Because forced volunteerism and even mandatory paycheck deductions for charitable causes are still a part of life in China, not everyone takes instantly to requests for charitable donations or volunteer efforts. But, odds are, if you set up a good volunteer or matching funds program and participate in it yourself, your employees will do the same—and they will be glad they did.

- **DON'T HIDE YOUR LIGHT UNDER A BUSHEL BASKET.**

  Serving the people should not be a cynical publicity ploy, but if your corporation is doing good works for good reasons, let this be known. Almost every CSR program has a public relations component, and many are run out of PR functions. Publicity for your service in China should be targeted not just at the Chinese press, public and government, but at your home market. Employees, stockholders, customers and elected officials at home also should know that you are doing everything in your power to be ethical and responsible in China.

- **CHARITY BEGINS AT HOME IN CHINA—BUT IS FAST EXPANDING.**

  Many foreigners look at China and see a country

that has only a nascent concept of charity and philanthropy. In fact, charity thrives in China, but it
has long been family and community based. Families provide many services that governments do in
the West. If a prospective college student and his
parents can't afford college tuition, they borrow it
from relatives; if a retiree needs heart surgery,
working relatives pay for it. That said, an increasing number of people have begun to donate to
domestic public charities, like Project Hope. The
Asian Tsunami also brought forth an outpouring of
donations from a populace that can increasingly
afford to be compassionate to those outside China
who are less fortunate. Charitable donations and
charitable work are likely to expand rapidly in
China in coming years.

- **CSR IS GROWING AMONG CHINESE CORPORATIONS.**
In the Mao era, state-owned enterprises literally
existed to serve the people—they provided employment, housing, education, medical care, and more
to their employees, with business itself almost a
sideline activity. Freed of these welfare obligations
when the market reforms began, most enterprises
were for many years more interested in the bottom
line than corporate social responsibility. However,
because of the current administration's emphasis on

putting people first and making development sustainable—not to mention the criminal corporate negligence that has led to an appalling work-related death rate and major environmental damage—corporations have come under increased pressure to behave responsibly. There is also a growing recognition that responsible social behavior will support efforts to go global and, we can assume, a genuine desire to be good corporate citizens. As Chinese corporations become more involved in CSR, more will be expected of multinationals.

- **INVESTIGATIVE WORK IS ESSENTIAL TO CSR.**
Investigative work is a key aspect of corporate social responsibility. It means making sure that all the companies in your supply chain are responsible businesses and ensuring that any organization to whom you contribute money or with whom you work is legitimate, honest, and likely to be around for the long run. It is also important to understand how the organization is perceived by the government and the press and to have a good sense of the strength of its relationships in these areas if you plan to parlay your service to the people into access or publicity.

NOTES:

We should be modest and prudent—"China's Two Possible Destinies," April 23, 1945.

Inspecting Official: Greetings Comrades!—in Wikipedia, "Serve the People."

China has inherited a backward economy—"Report to the Second Plenary Session of the Seventh Central Committee of the Communist Party of China," March 5, 1949.

Had Mao died in 1956—as quoted in Short, p. 629.

moved a nation...and changed the world and *I have not been able to change it*—Kissinger, *The White House Years*, p. 1063.

that little island and *asked the Japanese to return to their ancestral home*—as quoted in Spence, p. 178.

I have a very great defect and *I have long since learned*—"Letter to Peng Huang," January 28, 1921, in *Road to Power*, Volume II, p. 38.

I have met no one, with the possible—Kissinger, *The White House Years*, p. 1058.

In Chinese society today, educated—"A Fund-Raising Notice for the Shanghai Work-Study Mutual Aid Society," March 5, 1920, in *Road to Power*, Volume I, p. 498.

At examinations whispering into each other's ears—Schram, p. 205.

Because they have no commercial power—"Hunan Under the Provincial Constitution" July 1, 1923, in *Road to Power*, Volume II, p. 171.

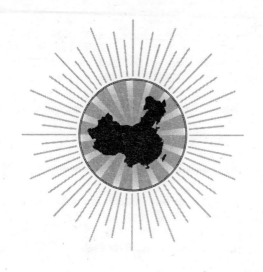

BIBLIOGRAPHY

BOOKS

Barme, Geremie R. *Shades of Mao, The Posthumous Cult of the Great Leader.* Armonk, London: M.E. Sharpe, 1996.

Becker, Jasper. *Hungry Ghosts, Mao's Secret Famine.* New York: Henry Holt, 1996.

Burr, William. Editor. *The Kissinger Transcripts.* New York: New Press, 1998.

Chen, Jerome. *Mao Papers, Anthology and Bibliography.* London: Oxford University Press, 1970.

Clissold, Tim. *Mr. China.* New York: Collins, 2005.

Doctoroff, Tom. *Billions: Selling to the New Chinese Consumer.* New York: Palgrave Macmillan, 2005.

Feigon, Lee. *Mao, A Reinterpretation.* Chicago: Ivan R. Dee, 2002.

Fernandez, Juan Antonio and Laurie Underwood. *China CEO: Voices of Experience from 20 International Business Leaders.* Singapore: Wiley, 2006.

Kissinger, Henry. *The White House Years.* Boston, Toronto: Little, Brown and Company, 1979.

Kissinger, Henry. *Years of Upheaval.* Boston, Toronto: Little, Brown and Company, 1982.

Li Zhisui. *The Private Life of Chairman Mao.* (Tran. Tai Hung-Chao, Ed. Asst. Anne F. Thurston) New York: Random House, 1994.

Macartney, Lord George. An *Embassy to China, Being the Journal kept by Lord Macartney during his embassy to the Emperor Ch'ien-lung, 1793*. 4. ed. J.L. Cranmer-Byng, London: Longmans, 1962.

McGregor, James. *One Billion Customers*. New York: Free Press, 2005.

Mao Zedong. *Poems*. Beijing: Foreign Languages Press, 1998.

Mao Zedong. *Report from Xunwu*. Trans. Roger R. Thompson. Stanford: Stanford University Press, 1990.

Mao Zedong. *Selected Works, Vol. I–IV.* Peking: Foreign Languages Press, 1967.

Mao Zedong. *The Writings of Mao Zedong*. Edited by Michael Y.M. Kau and John K. Leung. Armonk, NY: M.E. Sharpe, 1986.

Nixon, Richard. *The Memoirs of Richard Nixon*. New York: Grosset & Dunlap, 1978.

Pye, Lucian W. *Mao Tse-tung, The Man in the Leader*. New York: Basic Books, 1976.

Quan Yanchi. *Mao Zedong: Man, Not God*. Beijing: Foreign Languages Press, 1992.

Rittenberg, Sidney and Amanda Bennett. *The Man Who Stayed Behind*. Durham and London: Duke University Press, 2001.

Schram, Stuart. *Mao Tse-tung*. New York: Simon and Schuster, 1966.

Schram, Stuart. *The Thought of Mao Tse-tung*. Cambridge: Cambridge University Press, 1989.

Schram, Stuart R. *Chairman Mao Talks to the People: Talks and Letters: 1956–1971*. New York: Pantheon Books, 1974.

Schram, Stuart R., Editor. *Mao's Road to Power, Revolutionary Writings 1912–1949*. Volume I, The Pre-Marxist Period, 1912–1920. Armonk: M.E. Sharpe, 1992.

Schram, Stuart R., Editor. *Mao's Road to Power, Revolutionary Writings 1912–1949*. Volume II, National Revolution and Social Revolution, December 1920–June 1927, Armonk: M.E. Sharpe, 1994.

Short, Phillip. *Mao, A Life*. New York: Henry Holt and Company, 1999.

Snow, Edgar. *Red Star Over China*. New York: Grove Press, 1973.

Solomon, Richard. *Mao's Revolution and the Chinese Political Culture*. Ann Arbor: Center for Chinese Studies, University of Michigan, 1971.

Spence, Jonathan. *Mao Zedong*. New York: Lipper/Viking (Penguin), 1999.

Spence, Jonathan. *The Search for Modern China*. New York/London: W.W. Norton, 1990.

Tang, Jie. *Managers and Mandarins in Contemporary China, The Building of an International Business Alliance*. London and New York: Routledge, 2005.

Terrill, Ross. *Mao: A Biography*. Stanford: Stanford University Press, 2000.

Xiao Yu (Siao Yu). *Mao Tse-tung and I Were Beggars*. Syracuse: Syracuse University Press, 1959.

ARTICLES

Abramson, Neil R. and Janet Xi Ai. "Performance-Enhancing Strategies for China: Lessons from Japanese and American Companies." Carnegie Bosch Institute Working Paper 96.1, 1996.

"Addressing China's Looming Talent Shortage." McKinsey Global Institute, October 2005.

"American Corporate Experience in a Changing China—Insights from AmCham Business Climate Surveys, 1999–2005." American Chamber of Commerce-PRC and American Chamber of Commerce in Shanghai, 2006.

"Anti-monopoly push may hit Microsoft." Bloomberg.com. September 24, 2006.

Ashbrook, Tom. "China's Dot Communism." wbur.org, August 27, 2002. (see http://www.onpointradio.org/shows/2002/08/20020827_a_main.asp)

Barmé, Geremie R. "History for the Masses." in *Using the Past to Serve the Present*, edited by Jonathan Unger. M.E. Sharpe, Inc., Armonk, NY, 1993.

"Best Practices: Intellectual Property Protection in China." The U.S.-China Business Council (http://www.uschina.org/info/ipr/ipr-best-practices.html).

Bieman, Irv. "Strategy Management & the Talent Contradiction: An Alternative View on How to Catch Mice." (http://www.cbiz.cn/). October 12, 2006.

"Blogs on the Rise in China." *Shenzhen Daily*. October 18, 2006.

"Bribery involving multinationals rising." China Daily. December 12, 2006.

Brubaker, Richard. "An NGO Partner." China CSR.com, November 8, 2006.

Bush, George. "Speech at Boeing plant." Issues 2002.org. May 17, 2000.

Chan, John. "Beijing's new moral model: from peasant soldier to middle class consumer." World Socialist website, March 30, 2006.

Chan, John. "A grand ceremony for Confucius: Beijing turns to the old imperial ideology." World Socialist website, November 12, 2005.

Chandler, Clay. "China snubs foreign investment." *Fortune*, October 3, 2006.

Chandler, Clay. "The Great Wal-Mart of China." *Fortune*, July 25, 2005.

Chen, Mark Yu-Ting, Lincoln J. Pan, and Hai Wu. "Developing China's nonprofit sector." McKinseyquarterly.com, August 2006.

Cheng, Eva. "China: Capital 'invasion' sparks concern." September, 2006.

"China Could Become World's Largest Exporter by 2010." www.oecdchina.org. September 16, 2005.

"China Data: Trade and Investment Since 2001." *China Business Review*, September–October 2006.

"China Marks International Poverty Day." *Xinhua*, October 18, 2004.

"China Publishes Hu Jintao, Mao Zedong's Speeches on Hard Work, Arduous Struggle." *Beijing Xinhua* in English, June 18, 2004 (FBIS).

"China will not export revolution, development strategy official." *Shanghai*, September 21, 2006 (BBC Monitoring via COMTEX).

"China's most valuable brands released." www.china-embassy.org. June 20, 2006.

"China's People Problem." *The Economist*. April 14, 2005.

Chrastina, Paul. "Emperor of China Declares War on Drugs." http://opioids.com/opium/opiumwar.html.

Chua Chin Hon. "China: Enter the dragon, and beware the consequences." *The Straits Times*, September 24, 2004.

"Companies Speak: The State of U.S. Business in China." U.S.-China Business Council, 2006.

"Comrade Mao Zedong's Historical Role and Mao Zedong Thought—Resolution on Certain Questions in the History of Our Party Since the Founding of the People's Republic of China." (abridged). International Department, Central Committee of CPC, 1981.

"Consumer Preference Survey for UPS." Research International, http://pressroom.ups.com/chinasurvey/media/2005_china_sur vey.pdf, July 7, 2005.

"Constitution of the Communist Party of China (CPC) amended and adopted at the 16th CPC National Congress." *Xinhua*, Nov. 14, 2002.

"Conversation between Stalin and Mao." December 16, 1949. Cold War International History Project, Smithsonian Institution.(http://www.isop.ucla.edu/eas/documents/ma0 491216.htm)

Dai Yan. "Foreign takeover controversial." *China Daily*, April 11, 2006.

"Dell faces class-action lawsuit in China." *People's Daily Online*, August 4, 2006.

Deng Xiaoping. "Excerpt from a talk with the Japanese delegation to the second session of the Council of Sino-Japanese Non-Governmental Persons." June 30, 1984. (see http://english.peopledaily.com.cn/dengxp/vol3/text/c1220.html Deng Xiaoping)

Deng Xiaoping, "Speech Delivered at an Enlarged Conference of the Party Central Committee." February 6, 1962.

Dunn, Alison. "Behind the Chinese M & A Surge." *S & P Ratings News*, July 26, 2006.

Dyer, Geoff and Tom Mitchell and Sundeep Tucker. "Forbidden country? How foreign deals in China are hitting renewed resistance." *The Financial Times*, August 8 2006.

Ecke, Richard. "Success in training China's managers." *Asia Times Online*, July 29, 2006.

Fairclough, Gordon. "GM's partner in China plans competing car." *The Wall Street Journal*, April 5, 2006.

Fan, Maureen. "China's Party Leadership Declares New Priority: 'Harmonious Society' Doctrine Proposed By President Hu Formally Endorsed." *The Washington Post*, October 12, 2006.

Farrell, Diana, Ulrich A. Gersch, and Elizabeth Stephenson. "The value of China's emerging middle class." *McKinsey Quarterly*, June 2006.

Fei Yi. "CPC's Top Hierarchy Busy with Inspection Tours." China News Agency, May 17, 2006.

Feng Xianzhi and Jin Chongji (chief editors). Mao Zedong Zhuan, 1949–1976. (A biography of Mao Zedong). Zhongyang Wenxian Chubanshe, 2003.

Fischer, Bill. "China's Great Talent Contradiction." http://www.cbiz.cn. September 21, 2006.

"Following Instruction by Hu, 'Red Tour' To Be Launched in Mao's Birthplace." *Beijing Xinhua* in English, July 15, 2004 (FBIS).

"Foreign firms dominate China's exports." *Asia Times Online*, June 30, 2006.

"Foreign media urged to take just attitude towards China." www.china-embassy.org. May 16, 2005.

"40 percent Chinese cannot speak putonghua." *People's Daily Online*, September 5, 2006.

Fowler, Geoffrey A. "How blogging can galvanize China." *The Wall Street Journal*, January 19, 2007.

"French Presidents' China Complex," *People's Daily Online*, March 10, 2004.

Fulbrook, David. "China, an emerging charity superpower." *International Herald Tribune*. March 16, 2005.

Fullbrook, David. "The Red Chamber (of commerce)" *Asia Times Online*.

Gardner, Dinah. "The new People's Republic." *The Standard*, October 7, 2006.

Gomi, Ram. "China: Rule of law, sometimes." *Asia Times Online*, July 3, 2003.

Gross, Ames and Loren Heinold. "2005 Human Resources Trends in China." SHRM Global Forum, May 2005.

"Harvard professor's biography of Mao Zedong, big hit." *Xinhua*, April 7, 2006.

Heim, Kristi. "Microsoft out of China? Yeah, right." Tech Tracks, *Seattle Times*, November 2, 2006.

"High-tech products dominate exports of foreign-funded enterprises." *Xinhua*, January 28, 2006.

Hirt, Martin and Gordon Orr. "Helping China's companies master global M&A." McKinsey Quarterly.com, August 2006.

Hu Angang. "Guojia caifu: Mao Zedong dui dangdai Zhongguo shehui de yingxiang (A national treasure: Mao Zedong's influence on contemporary Chinese society)." *Guoqing Baogao*, No. 37, August, 2005.

"Hu: China must ease wealth gap." *China Daily*, July 6, 2006.

Hu Jintao. "February 19, 2005 Speech at Special Discussion Class for Principal Leading Cadres at Provincial and Ministerial Levels to Study Issues About Building a Harmonious Socialist Society." *Xinhua*, June 30, 2005 (FBIS translation).

Hu Jintao. "Remarks by Chinese President Hu Jintao to the U.S.-China Business Council, The U.S.-Chamber of Commerce, and The National Committee on U.S.-China Relations," April 20, 2006. (Transcript by Federal News Service.)

Hu Jintao. "Speech at Communist Party of China Forum on Mao Zedong's 110th Birth Anniversary." *Xinhua*, December 26, 2003 (FBIS translation).

Hu Jintao. "Speech at CPC Forum on Mao Zedong's 110th Birth Anniversary." Xinhua Domestic Service in Chinese December 26, 2003 (FBIS translation).

Ichiko Fuyuno. "Across China's Frontier." *Nature* Volume 439, Issue 7078, p. 781, February 16, 2006.

Jacob, Rahul. "Joint Ventures Struggle to bridge Cultural Divide." *The Financial Times*, March 27, 2001.

Jordans, Frank. "China gives Europe investment a wary eye." Associated Press, September 27, 2006.

Joseph, William A. "A Tragedy of Good Intentions, Post-Mao Views of the Great Leap Forward." *Modern China*, Vol. 12, October 1986.

Kahn, Joseph. "Where's Mao? Chinese Revise History Textbooks." *New York Times*, September 1, 2006.

Knight, Nick. "The Form of Mao Zedong's 'Sinification of Marxism.'" *The Australian Journal of Chinese Affairs*, No. 9.

Kundu, Swati Lodh. "China's impending talent shortage." *Asia Times Online*, July 6, 2006.

Kurtenbach, Elaine. "China Rethinks Foreign Business Policies." Associated Press, September 15, 2006.

Lague, David. "Selling in China? Which one is it?" *International Herald Tribune*, January 16, 2006.

Laing, Jonathan R. "What Could Go Wrong With China?" *Barrons*, July 31, 2006.

Lampton, David M. "Paradigm Lost." *National Interest*, September 1, 2005.

Lan Xinzhen. "Famous Brands Lose Face." *Beijing Review*, July 22, 2005.

Lavelle, Louis with Susann Rutledge. "China's B-School Boom." *Business Week Online*, January 9, 2006.

Lee, Don. "Job hoppers chase pots of gold." *The Standard*, February 23, 2006.

Levin, Richard C. "Speech at Conference on Sino-U.S. Educational Exchange," Nov. 10, 2003. (see http://www.yale.edu/opa/president/speeches/20031110.html)

Li Qian. "KFC sullies Chinese classic." July 14, 2006.

Li Weitao. "By design." *China Daily*, June 20, 2005.

Liu Guoguang. "It Is Time to Emphasize Social Fairness." *China Economist*. May 12, 2006.

Liu Wei. "Health Poverty Quite Serious in China." *People's Daily Online*, July 14, 2003.

"Local talent rises through ranks in foreign enterprises." *People's Daily*, December 18, 2003.

Long Yongtu. "Special Report: China II: Playing by the Rules." *Outlook Journal*, May 2006.

Luo Yadong. "Blending Cultural Business Styles." *MIT Sloan Management Review*, Fall 2002.

Mao Xinning. "Wode Yeye Mao Zedong (My Grandfather Mao Zedong). "Conversation on the Strong Country Forum of People's Web." (www.qglt.com).

MacKinnon, Rebecca. "China's Starbucks-blogger-gate: Hype and reality." Rconversation.blogs.com. January 22, 2007.

Macleod, Calum. "China's highways go the distance." *USA Today*, January 29, 2006.

Marquand, Robert. "China's media censorship rattling world image." *The Christian Science Monitor*, January 24, 2006.

Marquand, Robert. "Modern China's founding legend: heavy on myth?" *Christian Science Monitor,* May 22, 2006.

McGregor, James. "How China learned to love capitalism." *The Observer,* November 6, 2005.

Medeiros, Evan S. and M. Taylor Fravel. "China's New Diplomacy." *Foreign Affairs,* November/December 2003.

Melvin, Sheila. "Emperors' delight now the shame of China." *International Herald Tribune,* August 7, 2002.

"Microsoft Expects Bright Days in China." *People's Daily Online.* April 29, 2006.

Miller, Alice L. "A Superpower? No Time Soon." *Hoover Digest,* No. 2, 2005.

Mirsky, Jonathan. "Peking rains curses on its rebellious 'demons.'" *The Times,* December 6, 1995.

"New China Celebrates 56th Founding Anniversary." *People's Daily Online,* September 30, 2005.

"One Size Does Not Fit All." http:// pressroom.ups.com/china-survey/article1.html, September 2006.

Pan, Philip P. "Hu Tightens Party's Grip On Power, Chinese Leader Seen As Limiting Freedoms." *The Washington Post,* April 24, 2005.

"Panel Examines China's Economy." McKinsey & Company China Roundtable http://www.mckinsey.com/ideas/infocus/china/roundtable/profiles.asp.

"Party school journal warns against China's widening income gap." *Peoples's Daily Online*, September 21, 2005.

"Poor population in China fell from 250 million in 1978 to 23.65 million in 2005." Embassy of the People's Republic of China, www.chinese-embassy.org, August 25, 2006.

"Private firms powering the economy in China." *People's Daily Online*, September 22, 2006.

Quan Xiaoshu, Che Yuming, and Wang Mian. "China's parliament adopts corporate income tax law." *Xinhua*, March 16, 2007.

Rein, Shaun. "Blogging down in China." *Business Week Online*, July 27, 2006.

"Renmin Ribao Commentator on Carrying Forward Spirit of Xibaipo." *People's Daily Online*, June 16, 2004 (FBIS translation).

Roell, Sophie. "China's M & A misfortunes." The Banker.com, September 4, 2006.

Schwankert, Steven. "China Internet market grows to 137 million users." IDG News Service, January 23, 2007.

Selected Works of Mao Zedong, Volume III. Preface and Postscript to Rural Surveys; Preface, March 17, 1941.

Shen, Samuel. China's Wealthy Splurge $63 Million at Luxury Show in Shanghai Bloomberg, October 16, 2006.

Shobert, Benjamin. "The Brand New China." *Asia Times Online*, September 28, 2006.

Sisci, Francesco. "China's Revolution for Everyone and No One," *Asia Times Online*, October 21, 2005.

Sisci, Francesco. "Is China Headed For a Social Red Alert?" *Asia Times Online*, October 20, 2005.

Solman, Paul. "Reviving General Motors." "Online News Hour with Paul Solman," April 20, 2006.

Stakelbeck, Frederick W. Jr. "Beijing's 'separate but unequal' tax dilemma." *Asia Times Online*, March 28, 2006.

Starr, John Bryan. "'Good Mao, Bad Mao': Mao Studies and the Re-evaluation of Mao's Political Thought." *The Australian Journal of Chinese Affairs*, No. 16, July 1986.

Stiglitz, Joseph. "China's Roadmap," 2006. www.project-syndicate.org

Stiglitz, Joseph. "Development in defiance of the Washington consensus." *The Guardian*, April 13, 2006.

Sun Chengbin. "Sincere Wishes and Ardent Expectations—On-the-Spot Report on General Secretary Hu Jintao's Visits and Inspections in Yan'an During the Spring Festival" Xinhua Domestic Service, January 31, 2006 (WNC translation).

Tang Yuankai. "Mao Now." *Beijing Review*, October 5, 2006.

Teiwes, Frederick C. "Mao and His Lieutenants." *The Australian Journal of Chinese Affairs*, No. 19/20, 1988.

Terril, Ross. "Mao Now." *The Wilson Quarterly*, Autumn 2006.

"The Case of 'Super Voice Girl' Will Enter CEIBS Classroom." Ceibs.edu. September 29, 2005.

"The prospect of a powerful trading nation." *People's Daily Online*, January 10, 2005.

"The State Council has submitted the draft outline of the 11th Five-Year Plan." *People's Daily Online*, March 8, 2006.

Thomson, Clive. "Google's China Problem (and China's Google Problem)." *New York Times Magazine*, April, 23, 2006.

Tong Dahuan. "Government administrative monopoloy is corruption." *Beijing Youth Daily*, September 24, 2001.

Tsai Ting-I. "The latest China-Japan flap—cosmetics." *Asia Times Online*, October 14, 2006.

"2005 White Paper on American Business in China." American Chamber of Commerce in China and American Chamber of Commerce in Shanghai, September 1, 2005.

"U.S. warns China over rise of 'economic nationalism." *Taipei Times*, August 30, 2006.

UPS Survey Reveals Insights On Marketing to Chinese Consumers. Aug. 21, 2006. (see http://pressroom.ups.com/china-survey/pressrelease.html)

"Use Scientific Theories to Arm the Mind and Push the Work Forward—Roundup on Theoretical Building Since 16th CPC National Congress." *Xinhua*, April 19, 2006.

Von Morgenstern, Ingo Beyer, and Xiaoyu Xia. "China's high-tech market: A race to the middle." *McKinsey Quarterly Online*, September 2006.

Wang Yong. "China in the WTO: A Chinese View." *China Business Review*, Issue 5, 2006.

Watts, Jonathan. "China Chops Nike Ad." *The Guardian*, December 8, 2004.

Wiseman, Paul. "U.S. Companies profits take off in China." *USA Today*, October 25, 2006.

Womack, Brantly. "Where Mao Went Wrong: Epistemology and Ideology in Mao's Leftist Politics." *The Australian Journal of Chinese Affairs*, No. 16, July, 1986.

"Woman tops list of China's richest." China Daily (Reuters). October 11, 2006.

Wiseman, Paul. "U.S. firms' profits take off in China." *USA Today*, October 25, 2006.

Wu Zhong. "Beijing cracks the whip on rogue projects." *Asia Times Online*, August 22, 2006.

Xin Zhiming. "New corporate tax structure should do wonders for the economy." *China Daily*, March 20, 2007.

Xin Zhiming. "Unified corporate tax sign of progress." *China Daily*, March 9, 2007.

Yan Shuhan. "Special Column on Proposal for 'Building a Socialist Harmonious Society.'" *People's Daily*, June 17, 2005 (FBIS translation).

Yang Ruoqian. "Dramatic Increase in Chinese Youths' Average Height." *People's Daily Online*, June 19, 2002.

You Nou. "FDI quality under the microscope." *China Daily*, September 4, 2006.

Yuan Weishi. "Bingdian" special article by Zhongshan University Professor Yuan Weishi: "Modernization and History Textbooks." Zhongguo Qingnian Bao (*China Youth Daily*, Internet Version), January 28, 2006 (FBIS translation).

Zeng, Candy. "Chinese travelers' uncivil liberties." *Asia Times Online*, October 5, 2006.

Zhang Fan. "Maoxue: Guowai jian leng, guonei, zheng re" (Mao Studies: Turning cold abroad, getting hot in China). *New World Weekly*, April 3, 2006.

Zheng Bijian. "Ten Views on China's Development Road and Peaceful Rise and Sino-European Relations." China Reform Forum, December 15, 2005.

Zheng Bijian. "Path of Chinese cultural revitalization." *People's Daily Online*, September 26, 2006.

Zhu Xueqin. "Harmony stems from democracy." *China Daily*, December 12, 2005.

Zubok, Vladislav M. "The Khrushchev-Mao Conversations," July 31–August 3, 1958 and October 2, 1959 (see www.people.fas.harvard.edu/~johnston/Mao-Khrushchev.pdf).

INTERNET SITES

http://bfchina.de/

http://blogs.telegraph.co.uk/foreign/richardspencer/

http://english.cri.cn/critoday/events/mzd/index.htm

http://english.mofcom.gov.cn

http://homepage.mac.com/dwbmbeijing/iblog/SiHu/index.html

http://mzd.chinaspirit.net.cn/

http://news.imagethief.com/blogs/china/

http://rconversation.blogs.com

http://www.allroadsleadtochina.com

http://www.amcham-china.org.cn

http://www.amcham-shanghai.org

http://www.bjreview.cn

http://www.businessroundtable.org

http://www.cbiz.cn

http://www.chinabusinessreview.com

http://www.chinabusinessservices.com

http://www.chinabusinessservices.com/blog

http://www.chinacsr.com

http://www.chinadaily.com.cn

http://www.chinadevelopmentbrief.com

http://www.chinadigitaltimes.net

http://www.chinaeconomicreview.com

http://www.china-embassy.org

http://www.chinalawblog.com

http://www.danwei.org

http://www.diligencechina.com

http://www.hoover.org/publications/clm/

http://www.howardwfrench.com/

http://www.marxists.org/reference/archive/mao/

http://www.mckinsey.com

http://www.peoplesdaily.com.cn

http://www.rand.org

http://www.seeisee.com

http://www.sierraasia.com

http://www.uschina.org

http://www.wsws.org

http://www.zonaeuropa.com

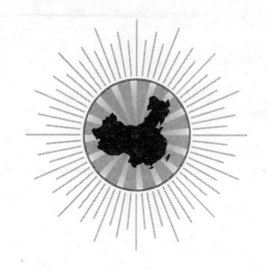

INDEX

ABOUT THE AUTHOR

Sheila Melvin is a writer and consultant who specializes in China. She spent seven years at the United States-China Business Council advising American businesspeople on the politics, economics, and practicalities of investing in China, and listening to their tales of woe and occasional triumph.

Ms. Melvin worked for the Council in both Washington and Beijing before establishing its first office in Shanghai. She spoke at numerous international conferences, including the Fortune Global Forum, and was elected to the Board of Governors of the American Chamber of Commerce in Shanghai. She contributed regularly to the *China Business Review* and freelanced for such newspapers as the *Wall Street Journal*, the *Asian Wall Street Journal*, the *New York Times* and the *International Herald Tribune*, writing primarily on culture.

Since leaving the Council, Ms. Melvin has continued to write about China and to take on select consulting projects. She is the co-author, with her husband Jindong Cai, of *Rhapsody in Red: How Western Classical Music Became Chinese*, which was short-listed for the Saroyan Prize in 2005. She contributes regularly to the *International Herald Tribune* and other publications, and is a member of the National Committee on U.S.-China Relations.

Ms. Melvin is a native of Washington, DC, and a graduate of the University of Pennsylvania. After college, she spent a year backpacking across Asia and was so enamored of China that, with $50 left to her name, she found a job teaching English in Taipei where she began to study Chinese. Her studies took her to Shanghai's Fudan University, where she was a student in the tumultuous spring of 1989. Ms. Melvin has an honors MA from the Johns Hopkins School of Advanced International Studies and was the recipient of the school's A. Doak Barnett Award for Excellence in China Studies. She has two small children and splits her time between the San Francisco Bay Area and Beijing.